My Three Encounters with God

Jesús Moreno

Printed in the United States of America

ISBN-13: 9781794382459

10 9 8 7 6 5 4 3 2

EMPIRE PUBLISHING

www.empirebookpublishing.com

Dedication

This book is dedicated to my wife Sue Prinzen, who was, is and will continue to be a pillar in my spiritual life.
"Life is a multi-colored event, in which the here and now only exist."
(Sue Prinzen R.I.P 7.12.15)

"If the common and ordinary man understood the mysteries of God, naturally he would be a species free of corruption and sin." Jesus Moreno.

IN MEMORY OF MY WIFE, SUE PRINZEN.

Contents

Acknowledgement

A special thank you to the people who without knowing me, believed in my talent as a writer. I cannot find words of gratitude towards these people, and the correct thing for me to do is to is say thank you to:

Francesca Maria (Editor)
Christy Anderson
Jorge Silva
Ricardo Ulloa
Jesus Bonilla (English/Spanish Editor)
Isidro Moreno and Ramona Camacho

Preface

This book recounts the testimony of its author Jesús Moreno. Jesús, now in his 50's is a humble man, who at the age of 7, longed to leave his home to explore the world. And one of his greatest wishes was to have a meeting with God. Jesús thought that by having an encounter with God, he would have the opportunity to ask him the fundamental questions, made to our creation. At that young age, Jesús formulated questions such as:

"Where do human beings come from?"

"Will there be life and resurrection after death?"

"Who is God and why did He create us?"

"Where does our knowledge originate?"

"Do the Angels exist and are they messengers of God?"

"Is our existence necessary in the universe?"

"Our spirit is matter?"

These are the kind of questions that, as a child, Jesús formulated. Although he did not know anything about Philosophy, Theology or Metaphysics.

Jesús never thought that when he asked himself those kinds of questions, he would become entangled in a life adventure without a fixed direction. On the waters of knowledge, the currents led him to empty into the vast ocean of philosophy. And in that vast ocean, Jesús sated his thirst for knowledge; he only hoped to have a meeting with God, to reaffirm what he had learned in the sea of knowledge.

During this search for knowledge and wisdom, the author discovered three ways to find God. The first form consisted of a traumatic event that took him to a near death experience, in this case, by an episode of hunger, thirst and physical disability. The second way consisted of the excessive use of the mind and its faculties. In this case study for long periods without enough sleep. And finally, the third way was produced by endless days of fasting and prayer in the mountains, which led him to have his last meeting with God.

After his three encounters with God, Jesús received the answers to all his questions, and what he learned is shared in this book.

And finally, if you believe that the Angels and the Miracles of God do not exist then today, I invite you to open your mind and be at home with reading the story that Jesús shares here. May the knowledge give you a definite meaning to your life. Jesús feels this testimony is a spiritual guide, in which you will find the answers to many of your questions, referring to your spirituality, and you will discover that believing in God is a genuine necessity, since we humans have a spirit and that spirit also needs to be fed.

"For every Philosopher, the search for the truth about the existence of God does not end after reading only one book. Because if that happens with the Philosopher, he will undress in his arrogance, and end up thinking, speaking, and reasoning like a primitive person." ~ Jesús Moreno.

Introduction

From the beginning, the creation of man has always had an unexplainable necessity to know, explore, and decipher the mysteries of his existence in this physical and metaphysical realm. And thanks to that inquisitive need, he began to speculate on its origins. Either he did it out of necessity, ignorance or madness. Today I can say with certainty, that inquisitive necessity that I carry within my being was what prompted me to write this book.

I want to add that the world of literature is composed of books, which have been published by eminent writers, some of these books contain myths and fables, also a bit of fiction. I want to affirm and confirm that my life and my story is not an exception. In this literary work, I will share the experiences of my encounters with God. These three encounters with God are the basis and foundation of my faith and my spiritual growth. After having witnessed, the Existence of God and His Angles I have in my hands the keys, to open the doors of the paradigm of knowledge.

Much of this book contains the theories of knowledge transmitted by God to man, which resemble the well-known ones, by eminent philosophers of all times. Although I know that the great Scholars of the world may criticize my theories presented in this book, I can only say; that God is the absolute omniscient and possessor of the truth, and not the Schools, Churches, Private Institutes or Universities founded by the primitive man.

With much humility, respect and simplicity, I leave this literary work in your hands, so that anyone can read it and share it with their loved ones. Especially, with all those brave ones like me, who decided to travel to the United States. Without more to say and add to this introduction, I will write my story, my memories, and my experiences; I hope that what I have written in this book is not offensive to you. What I would like, is that it reaches the deepest part of your heart.

"Our existence in a sub-world is governed by our dreams, thoughts, and ideas, which sometimes confuses our mind, creating moments of speculation, and confusion in our false reality, perceived by our senses." ~Jesús Moreno.

My Three Encounters with God

Chapter One

1. My place of birth.

For every human being, it is essential and indispensable, to speak with pride about the place where they were born, and I am not an exception. The environmental factors of that region played a significant role in my essence, my personality and my spiritual development.

After saying the previous thing, now I want to start by telling you a little about the place that saw me being born. I was born in Mexico, Distritio Federal, the Capital of Mexico, on a Sunday, March 29, 1970. My mother told me that I was born on an Easter Sunday. For her, my birth was special since I was born under a celestial event celebrated in all parts of the world - the Spring Equinox. I understand why, as a child, I have been disturbed by the divine things and their effects on humanity. The city of Mexico is considered one of the largest cities and overcrowded in the world. Its history goes back to the year 1300 AD, after Christ which was founded by the Aztecs on the lake of Texcoco. At that time, King Tenoch saw an eagle stand on a cactus devouring a snake. That was the signal he was waiting for from his Gods to establish the city of Tenochtitlan. 700 years after its foundation, now there are only hidden vestiges under a modern city. This metropolis has consumed its pre-hispanic wealth. It has revamped all of the buildings and peripheries, bringing with it a sea of unknown people, and have become one of the most dangerous cities in the world.

As proof of the dangers and obscurities of the city, I will write about an event that was held two years before my birth on October 2, 1968. "La Matanza de Tlatelolco" is well known in the history books of Mexico; a tragedy that was conceived of the worst atrocities committed by former President Gustavo Diaz. He gave the order to cowardly shoot a group of protesters opposed to its form of government. That day my parents walked by the outskirts of La Plaza de las Tres Culturas," and they were not aware of what happened nor did they participate in the alleged protest. The misfortune of being in that place almost cost them their lives. For them, that day, was a normal day like any other; they never thought that they would witness a tragedy. As they approached "La Plaza de las Tres Culturas," they noticed that there was military movement in all the streets.

Before arriving at the plaza, they decided to stop and entered a shoe store. Inside the store; they were informed of what was happening. The owner of the store told them that there was a protest and that the government of the state had sent for the military to attack and stop the protesters. The owners of the store told them not to leave because they had a feeling that something terrible would happen.

My parents took their advice and stayed inside the store. At that moment, the only thing they thought about was getting back home, but suddenly they heard sounds of helicopters flying over the area. From a distance, they saw the group of demonstrators, which was composed of teachers, students, workers, and families. The marchers were pacifists, but the President of the Mexican Republic took it as a revolutionary act against him. Without any dialogue, he gave the order to shoot down all the people gathered.

From above, the helicopters flew overhead with armed soldiers, ready to kill all the people gathered. It looked like a war camp as the streets were parading squads of soldiers and tanks of war with heavy artillery. Everything turned into total silence, and the soldiers

2

were waiting for the signal of attack. One of the crew members on one of the helicopters flashed a green light, which means "green light to shoot." At the moment, gunfire began, and people ran trying to protect themselves from the bullets, but for many of the congregation, it was useless. High-caliber bullets pierced their bodies; they fell bloody onto the ground where a sea of blood ran, shed by the victims. That was the most horrible thing my parents could have edured; it was like a scene from a war movie.

My parents did not leave the store until hours later, and they went home frightened, thinking about what happened with the wounded people. From that moment, my parents decided to move out of the city, and look for a piece of land on the outskirts of the city. Since that period of hostility from the governor to the students, he remained for several years in the city of Mexico. As a result of the tragedy forcing my brothers, Alicia and Juan had to give up their studies and dedicate themselves to work since all the students of the high school, college, and university, were threatened with death by the president of the Republic.

It is sad to know that a country can be marginalized of a high magnitude due to the ignorance of its leaders. Hopefully, this event taught us a lesson, and helps us recognize the stupidity of human beings and their complex superiority; we also hope that it will never repeat itself. I want to emphasize something very important; this message is not to express my political conviction about the government of Mexico, but use it as a reflection about the injustices that my parents, my brothers, and an entire generation lived through in 1968. The ravages and wounds provoked by these injustices will heal someday, but the people will never forgive such an atrocity.

After a misfortune of this magnitude, it only remains for me to say that the social problems of a country can marginalize a whole population, but something good and positive always comes out of the bad. Thanks to that tragedy, the genes of my parents were readapted to survival conditions. I inherited the best of them, and thus subsist above all imminent danger. I was born as an Aztec warrior, and I will die as such, fighting for the subsistence of my species, even if I accept specific Darwinian concepts related to the evolution of man. I wouldn't want to say that I've forgetten the mysteries of God and his divine grace over me, which means that God is my supreme creator, and he is absolute and necessary in my life. I have no more to say about my place of birth and do not want to add negative and uncertain observations of the beautiful country where I was born. I will go to the next stage of my life, which undoubtedly will be more interesting.

2.) My childhood.

While I was writing this book, I discovered what was important, which is the parenting that my parents gave me. With my hand in my heart, today I say that someday I would like to return to that place where I grew up to hug my parents and my brothers. And at that moment, I can recover the lost time and re-live the most beautiful moments of my childhood. I understand that stage of my life was crucial in my existence. With a lot of respect and pride, I will talk a little about my parents. I have always believed that an Angel of Light guided my parents, which took them from their hometown, Guanajuato, Mexico, and guided them to that magical place, called "Los Remedios Naucalpan. In that place, my parents found a good environment for my growth. There we became part of a community with its schools, churches, and recreational parks.

Everything was different in comparison to the big city. Here in Los Remedios, I studied elementary and some high school. In the back of my heart, I know that my first years of school were not as satisfactory as my parents thought. It was apparent that I was a little restless, playful, and naughty. Today, I remember with great happiness, those moments of my childhood when I played ball. I also remember those days when I bathed in the streams created by light rain. As well, as I have remembrance of the good, and the bad times, I lived in elementary school in my mind. I remember that I wasn't very applied, apparently, since childhood, my mind never rested as it generated ideas and thoughts out of reality. The bag of thoughts which had no meaning at that time was filled with questions of philosophical and controversial foundations.

The sad thing is to know that by that way of being and thinking, I would become an undisciplined child. Maybe I suffered from some medical condition, or perhaps I just asked my parents for attention. Whatever the cause of my personality, abuse and beatings are not justified as a method of correction towards an infant. Neither the beatings nor the insults changed my essence. On the contrary, I was looking for a way to be the best student in the school. Although I got bored in the classes, I tried in a thousand ways to understand why the classes were repetitive and basic. During my classes, I was the first to finish my assignments and exercises. When I got up from my chair, to help my colleagues, the teacher scolded me and sent me to talk to the school principal. I remember that the Director gave me ten swats on my ass. That was a form of discipline and punished me by having me sit in the corner of his office. A few hours after my punishment, the principal communicated with my parents to give them a complaint.

At the time, my parents found out about my bad behavior at school. When they returned home, they hit me with a belt. Maybe my parents did not understand that much of my boredom was because of the poor education that was in elementary schools in Mexico. I never understood why I was the one with the problem and not them. But I was content to think that my parents were not to blame either since they came carrying a chain of ignorance from previous generations. I think my parents did not understand my

5

situation, and try to solve the problem in an easy way. Instead, they blamed me for everything.

At that time, I had no knowledge of human behavior. I always agree with their methods of discipline and learning. I feel that my mind never tires and that it's continuously generating thoughts and ideas because God instilled that at the moment of my conception. Therefore, my mind is connected to the mind of God. And if God is the one who generates my thoughts and my ideas, that means that God and I are one in thought. And that is the reason why my mind will never rest.

While I am writing this book, I sit down to meditate and reminisce on my childhood, and it had come to mind, some memories of when I was in third grade. I remember that my teacher sat in the corner of the room next to a child who was more restless than me. The two of us always competed against each other to see which of the two finished the exercises faster. I must admit, that there was more than once that he beat me, possibly he was a child prodigy. I say this because he always answered all the questions of the teacher correctly. I also remember that same child, when he was doing his homework, he was going backward. It seemed that he was sitting in a rocking chair; his movement was contagious because it had rhythm.

That peculiar rhythm I still carry in my mind, along with its rare songs. I did not understand anything, but I liked to hear him sing. With his songs and his rhythm, I was telling myself, and I felt as if I was writing at the same speed as him. I did not understand why my subconscious made me see that child in a way different from other children. I came to think that I was inside that child. I got into his person and his behavior. I enjoyed playing with him during recess. One day, I noticed that he followed me everywhere, as if he were my shadow, sharing many experiences. It may be possible that I was the only one who could see him, and if any, he was a

6

reflection of me. In spite of everything I experienced at school and home, I loved playing with that imaginary friend.

That imaginary friend was a faithful companion for me who taught me many topics of life and the beginning of the universe. One of the main topics that I learned from him was our existence in this physical world is only an optical illusion. It is responsible for pleasing the will of the supreme creator. He told me that he lived within the spiritual reality of life, which contains one dimension more than our reality. He explained that our reality is composed of five dimensions. These five dimensions project to us the physical world in which we live, and our senses and our reasoning perceive that quality. He also added that the place where he came from is a capsule of time and space-gravitational. He assured me that live within that capsule is eternal and that its origins are compatible with the mind of God. I did not understand what he told me, but now that I am using reason, I can clearly understand what he was referring to.

One day, he came to my house to explore my surroundings - the hills and the springs of water. I remember, we walked among some bushes, and soon we entered a house in the form of an illuminated sphere; everything was white and it had some rare machines. He invited me to see his room. I followed him between several corridors, which have lots of lights and controls. When I was inside his room, I noticed something strange; he did not have any furniture except for a bed, and a big screen TV. Television was their means of communication with his parents, who were space travelers.

On the walls, there were decorations and symbols similar to the Egyptian hieroglyphics or Mayan codices. I asked him, "Do you know the meaning of the symbols?" He told me that he knew them because it is the ancient language of God. When he described the symbols to me, he spoke in a language unknown to me. He made some very strange noises like sound waves, which intrigued me more. I asked him, "What language is that?" He replied, "You just heard the universal language of God."

The moment he finished speaking about his language, I asked him, "You go to another school, right?" He told me, yes, but that his books were different from mine. I asked him to show me one of his books. Without hesitation, he took it out of his backpack. When I saw the book, I was surprised because its cover resembled none of my books; his book was just a screen. The title of the book, "The Creation of Man and the Universe," was translated from his native language. Suddenly, he moved the screen, and another book appeared. The second book title is "Before the creation of man." He told me that this book relates to the classification of living beings in the universe. And then he showed me a triangle in the form of a pyramid depicting entities and other beings, including man.

He noticed my amazement and explained, with great detail, the contents of the books. Each book contained site capitals. Its chapters were not very long in context. He suggested that I focus on the symbols because in them is true knowledge. The last chapter of the book titled, "The Creation of man," contained two summaries in the final pages. The chapters were prophetic; it was the revelation concerning the destiny of humanity. The books showed a new city, with a garden, and streets of stone and gold.

After reading his books, he invited me to see the flowers in his garden. We left his room and walked between corridors until we reached the garden. In the garden, there were a vast variety of plants, but the one that captivated me the most was a plant with exotic flowers. "Are those flowers roses?" I asked. He answered, "If they look like roses to you, touch their petals, and smell their aroma. When I smelled the roses, I realized that their fragrance was exactly the same aroma that I felt before he visited me. And so, it was a part of my childhood in the company of my imaginary friend. With which I lived an endless number of adventures, and I can say that I will never forget it. Just as I do not forget those beautiful moments when I used to go out for a walk in the countryside. My mind cleared, seeing the first rays of the sun furrowing the skies. I imagined that the same movement of the sun, our ancestors had observed it, day after day for thousands of years.

And of course, they documented it in stone calendars and hieroglyphics. How beautiful it was to hear the wild birds singing in the trees. I could just run over the dry grass, and feel its spikes dig into my bare feet. At the same time, I feel the wind hit my face; a cold wind with the morning dew spray. Every time my mind takes me to those moments of my childhood, my memory transports me to the past in a time machine.

And when transporting me in that time machine, my happy days arrive when my parents and my neighbors organized field day trips to "El Bosque de Los Remedios." That day I felt like a real explorer. I knew in advance that it would be a magnificent day full of adventures in the company of my family and friends. But most exciting of all was to walk on the aqueduct called "Los Arcos." Trees surrounded the ruins, and I liked to climb to the highest of the trees; reaching the highest point, I liked to contemplate the moon and the stars and to follow their course in the sky. Every time I climbed those trees, I imagined so many things that could have contributed to their surroundings.

At the same time, I was asking myself a million questions. "Why was the aqueduct built, what was the purpose of it? What was their purpose? Now those remnants are part of the forest and have been consumed by the habitation. It only remains for me to say that the new generations will miss the opportunity to organize field trips in the magic forest, and enter the ruins, or walk on the aqueduct. Los Arcos is an aqueduct that measures 50 meters in height and 500 meters in length. I walked it almost daily, and from the top, I could see the "El Cerro de Moctezuma." With its green trees and streams full of running water, this place is located between Los Remedios Naucalpan and Colonia Loma Colorada. To the visitor, there is a great enigma of the civilization that inhabited that place "The Culture of the Otomi," or also known as Tlatilco; this culture went out 13,000 years before Christ.

"Los Arcos Naucalpan de Juarez"(Picture from "RELATOS e historias EN MEXICO")

After crossing over the aqueduct, and into the forest. I ran without stopping until I reached "El Cerro de Moctezuma." Between my brothers and my friends, I always wanted to be the first to climb the cliffs, as I dreamed of finding the treasure that was hidden by Moctezuma. The natives of that place told me several legends of their ancestors. And one of those legends is that of Moctezuma and his family. The legend says that when Moctezuma learned that white men had arrived in their territories, they were exterminated the native Indians.

The King and his Family, accompanied by their priests, hid a treasure of great value in one of the hidden caves in the forest. I entered many of these caves, and I can say that they were elaborate. I also know that their length exceeds 3 miles. I was not the lucky one to find that treasure; nobody has found it, and still hidden in the labyrinth, waiting for someone to find it. The only given clue is that the caves are located under a church, which is now a Basilica.

Of all the legends that they told me, there was one, in particular, that was the most interesting of all. This legend captivated my ears, which I listened carefully so as not to lose any detail. They said, "In celebration of the end of the year, all the communities around the city met in the Cerro de Moctezuma to worship their Gods. And when they were all on the top of the hill, they formed a circle around a fire pit. The fire pit represented the sun, and the bodies dancing around it were the planets and the celestial stars. In the ritual, only their warriors and priests participated. The purpose of the celebration was to worship their Gods. During the celebration, they watched the stars to move from their position; it seemed that they received life. Suddenly, lights approached them, and they were flying objects in the form of spheres, which descended on the top of the mountain.

When the spheres landed on the ground, there were doors, and inside of them, rare beings came out, who were considered as Gods. These space travelers transmitted their knowledge to our ancestors. These legends are thousands of years old, which our ancestors passed them down, thus forming a tradition. They welcomed the Gods and interacted with them. The celebration lasted seven days, and every day, more beings descended from their ships. Many times, I doubted their stories and myths. Who hasn't heard unbelievable stories like this? It is speculated that since ancient times, our civilization has been visited by extraterrestrials. I believe that extraterrestrials have contacted most of us. But not all of us have perceived it, since they appear in disguise, in the flesh, so as not to disturb our senses or our body.

What unfortunate thinking, that man is the only intelligent being in the universe. Well, the truth will one day come to light, and all those myths will become a reality. For my part, I respect the traditions and culture of my ancient Mexico. How can I not to respect it if I am part of their culture and tradition? I proudly say that I am Mexican. And they will ask about "Cerro de Moctezuma," I will tell them that for the indigenous people the place was more than a sacred place. For them, it was the center of the universe, in which there is a window to other dimensions of outer space. And the long towers that are at the end of the aqueduct were built as astronomical observatories, and they align with Orion's belt. That constellation locates our position in the Universe. Is it a coincidence that they are in the same position as the pyramids of Egypt?

Listening to all those stories of the indigenous. I felt like a true explorer walking through the forest in search of a great archaeological treasure. I always walked very cautiously and paid close attention to my surroundings. Every object I found on the ground, I kept in a bag that I carried with me. No doubt that my mind was transported in time. Those were some of the stories, which I was fascinated listening to the natives, and sometimes I went alone to walk and explore the remains. I was a curious child that I felt very much within my being a have a huge attraction to the mystical of that place. Being there, I remained on my course to understand and record the information that was perceived.

The natives revealed to me more secrets of their ancestors which will be revealed in this work with the only purpose of transmitting the knowledge of a civilization that is in the process of extinction. Well, that was only a stage of my childhood. Thanks to the great support of my parents, I grew up being a healthy child. I also want to add that all those beautiful moments that I lived in their company; they were the key to the formation of my own being. And in a certain way, they were my motivation to go out and explore the world.

3.) My concern to go out and explore the world.

I desired to explore and conquer the world. It is an inherent need of every human being. During my childhood, my subconscious was collecting ideas and survival techniques to apply them in my adventure. This process was presented to me unconsciously every time I left a field trip day and played by pretending to be a child explorer. God himself was training me, and He was the one that aroused that curiosity of an explorer that I carry within my being. From an early age, God spoke to me in visions and dreams, and during one of those dreams, he advised me to leave my hometown. He let me know that is the only way that I could have a meeting with Him. One of the primary motivations in my life was the story of Jesus Christ. Watching His passion play out, my mind focused on the marvels that the son of God made here on earth in the company of his disciples. Since I am touching this religious theme, I will use it to write up the activities of the Holy Week, celebrated by the Catholic Church in the Naucalpan Remedies.

I remember that celebration. I always anticipated it because I knew beforehand that my parents would take us on a field trip the day after the ceremony. This tradition is known here as "The Passion of the Christ." Although it was nostalgic, it was difficult for me as a child to see how they beat and mocked Jesus Christ. But deep down I knew it was just a representation. I remember the faces of some of the actors and actresses, dressed in clothes of Roman soldiers of the time of Jesus Christ. I also remember people shouting to crucify Jesus. For some reason, my mind processed each event in detail, as if taking pictures, scene by scene, and archiving them into my memory bank. And now when I remember them, I relive each one of those images in my mind. I can still perceive the smells of the flowers, the sounds of whips, and the colors of the clothes worn by the actors. It also comes to my mind, the moments when they punished the person who personified Jesus Christ. I saw the way they relentlessly beat him with a leather whip, leaving wounds and marks on his back. People were pulling at him and ripping his clothes; they even stuck a crown of thorns on his forehead, and I saw the blood pour down his face.

Then, as he complained of intense pain, he was ordered to carry his wooden cross; I saw how his body movement stopped, as he fell to his knees hitting the earth with the tip of the cross. Some of the spectators spit in his face and beat him; I felt the pain in my back every time they whipped him. I remember asking my mother, "Why did they hit him so much, Mom? And why didn't anyone help him?" She told me with a firm voice that no one could help him because that's why he came to the world, to die for our sins. Well, with the passage of time, I understood that it was only a re-creation of Christ's passion according to the Holy Bible. In the end, this work inspired me, knowing that Jesus Christ was a missionary, a leader, and a savior, and I wanted to be like him even if it cost me my life.

As a child, I always thought that the world does not have any owner but God and that human beings are free to travel to all corners of the earth, without restrictions or having to have a passport. And for this reason, I told my friends and brothers, that one day I would go out to conquer the world. It's a bit ironic because even though I had everything in my house, I felt that I needed something more. Maybe it would be the satisfaction of saying I achieve something in life. I did not know what it was; perhaps it was an irrational impulse bigger than my willpower.

I knew that my mother did not like that I thought that way, but I told her that neither she nor anyone could prevent the will of God. At my young age, my mind had already programmed itself to go out and explore the world. As part of my preparation, I went out to walk to the Bosque de Los Remedios. I remember that my mother rejected my request to go, and then she kissed me on my forehead. "You don't want to be alone in the streets," she told me in a mocking

14

tone, "Better go play with your brothers." That was my mother's way of wanting to suppress my explorer's dreams.

Those words that she told me, I carry in my mind, and I remember them as if it had happened yesterday. For those same reasons, I held to my ideas until I thought it was the right time to leave my house. To calm myself down and calm my desperation, I left my home and went to visit my cousin, Gabino. He lived next to my house, and he accompanied me to walk along Bosque de Los Remedios. This act of going out to walk to the forest at night gave us a guideline to analyze the risks and dangers that could arise in our path toward the United States of America. My cousin was the one who encouraged me and told me that he would accompany me on my adventure. Knowing that I had the support of my cousin, I was excited, and my imagination flew. My mind created images of cities in a science fiction movie.

Three years after I planned my departure, my anxiety to leave my town to explore a new world made me crazy, and day by day, the concern became stronger inside me. I do not deny it. I also felt a little afraid, and my heart was filled with sadness with the thought that I was disappointing my parents with my actions, but even that would not change my mind. While I was still waiting for that day to arrive, I tried to live a normal life. I never stopped working because I needed to save enough money for my trip.

I worked at a tennis club during weekends, which was a way to earn money and to be able to help my mother with the expenses of the house. I knew that helping her was not my responsibility, and I never said anything negative about it. I do not deny it. I also lived moments of happiness and joy with my family, and I remember that day. After returning from my work, I accompanied my older brother. At a party, my brother and his friend, Angel, were DJ's that night. One hour after starting, a large number of young people gathered at the party, and all were getting carried away by the

15

music and dance without stopping as my brother tried to share the best Disco music of that time.

During the afternoon, while all of us were present, a spherical object on the outside appeared in the direction from the West to the. El Bosque de Remedios The unidentified object produced an intense light on its exterior. I heard my brother speak from the microphone, saying, "Greetings to our friends, the extra-terrestrials, who are passing through here." We all turned at the same time to look at the sky, trying to locate the flying object. That object was slowly decelerating as it was approaching us and was about a hundred meters high.

The object came so close that its brightness blinded our sight; after a moment we contemplated what we were seeing; it was merely suspended right above us for a moment. It felt as though time stopped. After a few minutes, the object continued its trajectory, at a slow speed of approximately three to five miles per hour, suddenly it accelerated towards El Cerro de Moctezuma.

My friend Ismael and I ran towards the hill, to be able to see the spaceship closer, as I approached the hill my legs felt heavy, and suddenly I was very fatigued with unimaginable exhaustion. As we approached the circle of the hill, the only thing we could see, were three beings who descended from the light. I tried to control my nerves and stay still so as not to attract attention, but apparently, they perceived our presence. They turned around in our direction, and I dropped to the ground so they would not see me, but after a while, I lifted my head to observe them. They held in their hands some articles resembling books or a stone box, which emanated a pure white light.

Suddenly I heard a strong swoon and fell to the ground, I lost consciousness for a moment, but upon awakening, the spaceship was moving away very quickly towards the sky and soon disappeared. How exciting and surprising was that experience? Until today that event was recorded only in my mind. My whole life

I had not found a logical explanation for this type of phenomenon, but now after my three encounters with God, my mind has expanded immensely, to help me understand this type of paranormal phenomena. And after confirming that we are not the only intelligent beings in the universe. This knowledge gives me a bit of tranquility in my existence since that shows of my being that I already passed that stage of ignorance.

Chapter Two

Getting ready to travel to the United States.

Based on my Christian-Catholic of faith, and the religious beliefs taught to me by my parents. I made a promise to the Virgin of Guadalupe, a few months before leaving my house and traveling to the United States. Which was the following; I would let my hair grow all year, without cutting it at all; in exchange for the Virgin to take me healthy and well to my destiny. And the way that I will repay my promise to the Virgin of Guadalupe would be as follows; climb on my knees to his Basilica located on the hill called "Cerro de Tepeyac." Twelve months passed after my promise, and I felt that the day of my departure was very close. And I began my preparations.

Now my dream of leaving home would become a reality, and I had already saved a little money, which was enough to cover my train ticket and my extra expenses. When I told my cousin that I already had enough money to travel, he said for me to think about it very well, because I was underage, and that could cause problems with my parents. He also warned me about the dangerous things that are happening on the border. I perceived that what he intended was to discourage me, but his comments did not change my mind. I told him that I was determined to travel, and I would do this with or without his help, I would leave my house the following Monday.

Finally, my cousin understood that I was not joking and that my decision was firm. No more discussion, respect was acknowledged. We stayed for the weekend together, to plan everything, we had already set the date of departure. And the perfect day was Monday as it was the start of the week. I preferred to leave that day because my older brothers and my parents usually worked. The preparation for my departure was a study of the habits of my relatives, only then everything would go well.

From that day I began to write a letter to my parents, which I would leave with my friend Lorenzo. I explained to him what I had planned with my cousin, and instructed him to send the letter a day after my departure. For me to leave without warning my parents was the right thing at that moment because knowing the characteristics of my mother; I knew she would oppose my decision. Three days before my departure, the Friday after my work; I visited my cousin. And I asked him to accompany me to El Cerro de Moctezuma for the last time. I was explaining to Gabino, my cousin, why I wanted to go to that place; I told him that a supernatural force compelled me to climb that hill.

(Notes on Cerro de Moctezuma: "It is a hill located in the municipality of Naucalpan, west of Mexico City. It is an archaeological zone protected by the National Institute of Anthropology and History and was part of the National Park of Los Remedios. It is one of the last green areas within the urbanized area of Naucalpan." -Source: Wikipedia)

First of all, I explained to Gabino that Cerro de Moctezuma is sacred to me, and also to every indigenous community of this place. Every time I climb to the highest part of the hill, I can feel the presence of the Ancient Gods. The God who identifies himself as "Quetzalcoatl" a pure white god full of light and whom allegedly descended from inside a luminous spaceship, to communicate with the natives of that region. My cousin inquired of me, "What mysterious forces makes you climb up to that place?" I replied, "I don't even know."

"But inside my mind, I answered in silence, this energy of attraction that I feel towards that place is produced by an intra-rational necessity, which exists in my Spirit since before my conception. My will and Spirit is merely a Divine attraction to God.

19

Well, whatever the reason, I thought that Man could not live without a supreme being that governs destiny and eternity. So every time I visited that place, I found an energy source more significant than my own will, which made me feel good, and it helped me to connect with plants, trees, and water, etc ... How beautiful it was to connect with nature in that way. When my mind entered that ecstasy, time and space ceased to exist.

After I explained to my cousin why I was visiting this particular hill, he finally agreed to accompany me to walk through the forest and up the mysterious green hill. That night the brightness of the full moon was in all its splendor and its light reflected on the water of the dam. A few hours after crossing much of the forest, we finally reached that sacred place. When we arrived on the hilltop, we sat down on some stones, which have sacred writings engraved on them. And they are similar to those I saw in my imaginary friend's house.

After we admired the stars, we walked towards an hill plateau (an area with a flat ground). And we began to dance in the same way that the indigenous people did. After dancing, we threw ourselves on the dry and arid ground and gazed at the sky. That night, it was a clear night without clouds, it seemed that God allowed us to feel and enjoy nature and all its splendor. I had the feeling that the universe is intelligible, and that God realized our purpose, to connect us with a life force - nature. God allowed us to enter into his metaphysical mysteries, where the reason, the senses and the intra-rational are united and become an emanation of energy.

Little by little the hours went by, and we did not stop laughing as we remembered anecdotes of our childhood. Which were many, of all those memories that we shared and laughed about, was once when my cousin Gabino liked a neighbor of ours, her name was Andrea, at that time my cousin and I were about ten years old. One night my cousin invited me to serenade Andrea. I accompanied him, and although I did not sing, I tried to make my voice sound like Pedrito Fernando, a professional singer, he sang very well, as a child in love - I sang the song like him. When I finished singing, Andrea came out of her house and kissed me, thinking that I was the one who had brought her the serenade. My cousin just smiled and said, "Let's get out of here."

Well, that was one of the childhood memories that we laughed about that night. The hours passed slowly, and the need to say goodbye to the Virgin of Guadalupe became more grounded within me. By the early hours of Saturday, after returning from the hill. My cousin and I decided to go to the Basilica de Guadalupe, to deliver my offering to the Virgin. Before boarding the bus, we went to get a steak sandwich at a lunch stand. After eating our breakfast, we boarded the bus in the direction of the "Cuatro Caminos."

We had asked a security guard about which bus to take because we didn't know the way to the Basilica. The security guard told us to board the subway in the direction of Villa Basilica; of the route number six.

When arriving at the Basilica and marveling over the beautiful architecture, l began to think deeply about all the things I knew and the things I didn't know yet. I was suddenly transported back in time, back to that day when the history of the Virgin's appearance. The day was December 9, 1531, at that time that place was still a pyramid built by the Aztecs. Its surroundings were desolate land with very little vegetation. I imagine that for the proselytes it was terrific to walk towards the top of the pyramid. But after the appearance of the Virgin the story changed entirely and on that pyramid or hill of Tepeyac, the Basilica dedicated to the Virgin was conceived.

Now, the Mexican people congregate in Tepeyac to worship the mother of God, and for many years, they stopped worshiping the Gods of the Aztecs. To be more accurate in the description of that breakthrough, I will describe it in the following way, according to the story. Juan Diego went to walk on the hill of Tepeyac and being on the top of the hill on December 12, 1531. The Virgin of Guadalupe spoke with him, and after talking with Juan Diego she set her picture in the throw-over what Juan Diego wore that day; well, there are more details of the story which I will omit as not to confuse the reader.

As I continued on my way, I reached the stone stairway that would take me to the top of Tepeyac. I thought that it seemed appropriate to fulfill my promise. At first, I placed my offering of roses on the floor, and then I rolled up my pant legs and got on my knees. Being ready and on my knees, I began to worship and sang some praises that my mother taught me as a child, I raised my eyes to the sky and started my journey. My senses were utterly perceptive to everything around me. The stone stairs carved by natives are the essential components of this fantastic place, each step decorated with artistic ceramic. They give the impression of being the entrance to a castle, also stretched from side to side of the stairs, arches well executed and carved by the natives. And then there are the plants with beautiful flowers, which gives a unique touch to the gardens of Tepeyac.

As I climbed up the stairs, my knees were bleeding from the rough floors that skinned my knees. When I reached the first section of the gardens, I stopped for a moment to contemplate part of the hill. After a few moments of rest, I knelt again and continued with my procession, the sound of water streaming from the waterfalls, distracted my mind from the pain, and I reassure myself, I had little time to reach my destination. It was not easy to get on my knees, but I could not stop.

To deliver my offering was very important, since this would help me to be a person of my word and determination. When passing through the park of the offerings, I looked to the bottom to see a chapel. That's where I had started my journey, I could not believe how many steps I climbed on my knees... and the road continued ahead, a few meters from where I stopped, to encounter the statue of the Virgin de Guadalupe. In that place, she is adored by a group of Aztecs.

When I reached the top of the hill I entered into despair; my body trembled with emotion and tiredness. As I looked at the doors of the chapel in front of me, I tried to stand up, but I could not. For me, they were like seeing the gates of heaven, where the Virgin of Guadalupe was waiting for me. Upon entering the chapel, I asked my cousin for help to get off the floor. He lifted me with both hands, I stood up and loudly shouted, "Here I am, Virgencita de Guadalupe, I'm here to deliver my offering to you." I walked a little closer to the place of the offerings, I prepared my cousin to cut off my hair, and I pulled out some scissors from one of my pockets. I gave my cousin the scissors and tied my hair with a rubber band; I bowed in reverence to the Virgin. Suddenly, there was total silence and only the sound of scissors cutting my hair, at the same time my eyes filled with tears. My cry was of joy, and I never thought that it would cause so much emotion.

Lady of Guadalupe at Cerro del Pepeyac

I took my freshly cut braid in my hands, lifted it up to the sky and I said to the Virgin; "I paid my promise to visit this sanctuary." My cousin approached me, by my side, and hugged me tightly saying; "The Virgin would protect us on our journey." Now, if I felt ready to leave my country. I felt a supernatural force take over my mind and my body and my soul. I did not know how to control my emotions, and the only thing I could do was contemplate the image of the Virgin.

Afterward, my cousin and I return home, to finish the preparations for the trip. Finally, we arrived early Monday morning to my cousin's house. I asked him if he was ready to leave. He gave me a signal, and we walked into his house. I felt a chill that shivered through my body; I do not know what kind of emotions this was creating, whether it was fear, joy or sadness. But in the end it was time, I felt great remorse and came to think I was betraying the trust of my parents. With all the pain in my heart, I said goodbye to my mother. I had to lie to avoid suspicion, and I told her I would return later than usual. I can already imagine the anguish of my mother, to not see me return home after many days have passed.

My plan went perfectly. We arrived without incident to the U.S border. For the State of Nuevo Laredo Tamaulipas Mexico., that same day we attempted to cross the border, but the Customs Agents arrested us more than once. Our attempts continued for several days. Seeing how difficult it was to cross the border, we decided to ask my uncle, Jose for help. Jose is the father of my cousin Gabino; my uncle sent us a message saying; that he would not pay for our trip, that it was better to go back home. I ignored his instruction, and I clung to my intentions to cross the border, my cousin decided to return to Mexico City. My cousin did not care that I was a minor and left me alone in the most dangerous border of Mexico. I did not want to return home defeated, for me it was more than a challenge to go to the United States. I was not afraid of losing my life in the intent. The months passed, and finally, I abstained to cross by myself.

Chapter Three

First encounter with God in the U.S border.

It happened in the year of 1986 on the border between Mexico and the United States. I was heading towards the desert aimlessly; thinking about the possibilities of surviving this trip, even though my hopes were not very encouraging since many people have died on the road. Knowing how dangerous it is to cross the border, I tried to be optimistic about it, and I never regret having reached that place.

After my cousin returned to Mexico City, I crossed the border with a group of people from the train station. It was a Friday night when we decided to cross the border. We walked for a few hours through deserted places, and at nightfall, we hid among some bushes. Suddenly, we heard a helicopter approaching us; frightened by the noises, we ran in all directions. I hid among construction waste, and I stayed there until dawn. When I saw the first rays of the sun, I left my hiding place and walked a little to look for my guides.

I searched for several hours. I walked many kilometers, and I never found them. Without knowing which direction to walk, I continued my trip, during the day the course of the sun guided me; and in the night, by the trajectory of the moon and the stars. At that moment, I put my explorer's instinct to the test. The first two days of the road, I thought that I only had one day to find a town or city. But the days passed, and I did not see any signs of life by any side. My food rations and the water were about to end. I continued walking between the valleys and mountains. The hours and days passed, it was already the seventh day of my journey, and I didn't

26

see houses anywhere. My eyes only saw desolate valleys, desert sand, and dry bushes. Tiredness invaded my body, my feet folded as I walked, and my hands trembled uncontrollably.

I felt weak and was about to lose consciousness; my food and water were gone; my body began to weaken more and more. In the distance, I saw an oasis of water and vegetation, but when I got close to that place, everything moved from its position, and the same reflection of water was far away. The hunger and thirst that I felt provoked hallucinations, at that moment, I wanted to be with my family, sitting in the dining room my house, enjoying company, and have dinner with cold lemon water. I sensed my death approaching. There was nothing else to do without food and water. I just closed my eyes, and I collapsed to the ground. I crawled on the sand to get under some bushes. I asked God to help me get out of that place. I drew up the strength from within, got up and continue walking. I did not walk much before feeling weak again and fell onto the hot sand.

I lost control of my mind and entered into a state of delirium. Without thinking about what I was saying, I cursed the name of God, and at the same time, I asked him, "What did I do to deserve to die in this place?" I understood that it was useless to blame God. I was the one who decided to venture out. I spent hours and hours asking God for forgiveness for the sins that I committed toward my parents and toward my fellow human beings. He did not respond to my prayers, but I never lost faith in him, and swear to give testimony of his existence.

The hours passed, and I remained in the same place. I raised my voice again to ask God for a miracle. "Lord, all-powerful creator of all that is visible and invisible, take pity on me, who am your servant. Command an army of Angels in my help, just as you guided the Hebrews when they left Egypt. I ask you to take pity on me, and you are the one to take me out of this place. After saying those words, I unconsciously raised my eyes to heaven and saw a glow of light overhead that was extremely bright.

I tilted my head to look at the floor, but I could not keep myself in that position. My eyes remained fixed and firm in that mysterious light. The energy emanating from the cloud penetrated my body, and I felt an electric shock going through every part of my being; from one moment to another my body froze, and when I was about to fall to the ground, I heard a deafening sound in the distance, which made me feel dizzy and made me fall to the ground. As I collapsed onto the ground, I felt desperate and wanting to run. But my effort to escape was useless since the light and sound kept me immobile. My body tensed, and my eyes cried tears of blood. After a few minutes of torture, I could no longer resist, and let that supernatural force take control of my mind, my body and my soul. There was nothing else to do about it; I felt inferior before such a powerful force.

Suddenly, I heard the voice of a man mention my name and said so, "Jesus, your time has come to depart. Today you will come with me to the kingdom of God." Hearing the words of that man, I felt as if I were dying and my mind returned to my childhood. I saw myself as a seven-year-old boy. I was celebrating the 12th of December, and Mexicans celebrated the day of Virgin Guadalupe's appearance. I walked on the dark streets, and in the narrow alleys of my neighborhood; my being filled with joy seeing the place where I grew up.

When I arrived in front of the altar of the Virgin, I knelt down and palmed my hands together to pray. I asked the Virgin for forgiveness for my sins, I also asked for my family's wellbeing. A few minutes after praying, the image of the Virgin came to life and descended from the altar. To see her beauty in all its splendor was beyond amazing. She opened her hands and took me in her arms. Then she spoke in my ear, saying, "Let's walk together so you can eat, drink, see, talk, listen and caress everyone you know." You have to do it right now because when you enter the paradise of God, you can't do these things anymore.

The Virgin took me by my hand, and we walked on a path toward a sacred place. We passed in front of the house of Mrs. Ra-amona, then we entered that mystical place seemed to be a temple. In the patio of the temple, fires were forming a circle. In the middle of the fires, I saw a column of rock erected toward the sky, and from the peak of the rock, a white dove descended. Jesus Christ was on the side of the rock. He spoke with a man who had a water jar in his hands. Christ said, "You will be my successor who comes after my era, and your paths will be like pure, crystal clear water, which comes from the heavens, and joins the rivers and seas of the earth. I continue walking in the company of the Virgin, I noticed that around each campfire, there were groups of people talking and eating.

In the first fire pit, I saw a group of children eating bread, accompanied by an Angel. They played with each other and threw stones inside the fire. In the second campfire, there was a group of young people, also accompanied by an Angel, they were singing and everyone had a glass of wine in their hands. And finally, in the third campfire, were all my relatives, friends, neighbors and adult people who have already died. My grandfather, Temu, dressed as an Angel of God. When I saw him walking with the Virgin, he approached me, and I sat at his right side. Then he told me, "Our existence is a reflection of the eternal and has three stages, yesterday, today and tomorrow. And these stages are as you see it; the conception, the present life, the death, and resurrection." He added, "Never try to rush your journey because the timing of God is perfect." I did not understand that concept of life, but I thought that my grandfather was right in what he said to me because he was already in the metaphysical realm.

When my grandfather finished speaking, I went back to see the Virgin, and she just smiled. After listening to my grandfather, my

29

deceased friends also talked with me. They looked in a normal state; I saw them drinking, eating, laughing and crying. I asked the Virgin, "Is this the paradise of God where the living coexists with the dead?" Will it be wise for me to speculate and realize that our reality is in dreams? And if my speculation was right, I could add, our mind is awakened in our dreams where the metaphysical world in its pure essence governs reasoning. It requires a moment of perception to locate itself in its second reality, which is in the physical world. And this reality is governed by your senses, as well as by your faculty of discernment.

That physical reality is only a phase to prepare the body, nourish it, and purify it. And after this preparation, the mind returns to dreams, where it connects with God, and there is where you can interact with the dead. The Virgin answered, "What you have seen and felt in my company is only a reflection of what exists in the Kingdom of God. Only that your physical body can't enter the metaphysical world, but when dying, you may not realize that you have died, and you think that you continue to occupy your body, but 24 hours later, you will no longer feel that sensation, and your spirit will be free for the resurrection."

In other words, the Virgin said; "In the resurrection, your spirit will be detached from your body, and will be reunited with the spirit of God. Until then, understand were my words, I cannot tell you more things about paradise. The job of explaining and guiding you through the tunnel of light is up to the man who just pronounced your name. He is your Angel who has been accompanying you from the moment of your conception. His name is Gabriel." Before saying goodbye, the Virgin gave me three roses, one white, one red, and one blue; later she allowed me to touch his green mantle full of vibrant stars. Then I saw how she returned to her altar and stayed there to comfort other captive souls.

Suddenly, I smelled roses, and an Angel appeared in the sky on a cloud. When the Angel descended from the cloud, he was accompanied by two other angels. The three Angels wore white and purple; their eyes were like two sapphire stones. Their hair was white as snow, and in his right hand he carried a cane, and he wore golden sandals. The Angel came directly toward me, took me by the hand, and with the help of the angels that accompanied him, they lifted me from the sand. The angels held in their hands a couple of roses. And when I smelled the pleasant aroma, I remembered the days when I accompanied my mother to the village church. After the Angel hugged me with tremendous strength, I felt a burning heat inside my being. Suddenly, he said, "Let's walk together because this is the time that your spirit will come before the foreknowledge of God, and He will decide if you will enter His Kingdom."

We continued walking directly to the entrance of the tunnel of Light. The Angel ordered me to stop to observe something. I stopped, and He pointed out three stones; one of them had the shape of a cube, the second was a bright white sphere, and in the third, were two triangles intertwined. After I observed the figures, he asked me, "Do you recognize these figures?" I replied, "Yes I do," and I gave him the description of each one of the stones. The Angel took out a vessel full of myrrh oil and anointed the three stones. We continue forward in the direction of the tunnel, which was high in the sky. The Angel told me," God has chosen you from the womb of your mother, and at the moment of your conception, he enabled you with the faculty of reasoning and also gave you the use of conscience, which you can call intra-rational. What I tell you is true, because I accompany you at that moment, when God equipped your body, mind, and soul with all their gifts and faculties."

"And so it happened the way you were equipped, God commanded me to take you to His paradise, to equip your soul with the necessary virtues and qualities, which will distinguish you from all other beings. And to your essence, I add intelligence, and most important of all, with feelings. After that process, I will take you on a trip to three places. The first, where you were born, the second, where you have grown, and the third, where you will die. You will see an essence of your present, your past, and your future. But at birth, you did not remember anything because your mind was forced to forget certain details of your existence. If you are able to recognize places and past events, your mind will tell you that it is only a dream. And your mind will be confused when trying to decipher the mysteries of God, and some events and places, are revelations of his Kingdom."

"God loves you so much that he gave you free will, to discern and investigate his mysteries. Apart from all your soul or your spirit, you can leave your body every night to connect with God's thoughts while you sleep."

"What do you mean by this? I ask. The Angel answered me, "God has equipped you with consciousness since before you were born because your soul comes from the essence of God, and was sheltered in paradise, waiting for the moment of your conception. And your Soul, by uniting with your body, activates its survival properties. Starting this way the intra-rational and intellectual knowledge, also your senses were enabled so that at birth you can perceive the physical world that surrounds you.

Suddenly the Angel stopped talking, and with his hand pointed down, we were rising toward the sky. From high up, I saw my body faint on the sand accompanied by the two Angels.

I could not conceive what my eyes were seeing. My spirit had abandoned my physical body, and my spirit occupied another radiant body full of light, but it was similar to the physical one with the same physical characteristics. The observer saw the observing; this was something unattainable for my mind. When arriving at the entrance of the tunnel, I felt a very strange sensation in my new body. I felt a wave of energy emanating from the tunnel. And that strength, my body, I continue to walk next to the Angel. In the distance from the inside of the tunnel, I saw a pair of hands, which move. They were the hands of a Being sitting on a throne.

Behind that radiant being, there were two women; one of them dressed in green and had the symbol of a throne drawn on her forehead. The second woman wore purple and had the symbol of a cup drawn on her forehead. As we made our way to the throne, I saw a flash of light that blinded my eyes. Inside that glow, I saw a hand that was extricating itself and trying to touch me. The Angel said to me, "Son of man, you are facing God. He is your only true God who punishes with an iron scepter." When the Angel said that, I fell to the ground. I did not understand because I felt fear before God. Suddenly, I felt my body heat up, like a red-hot iron. The hands of God lifted me from the ground, and its heat was like flames of fire coming from the Sun.

My body sweated and stopped, and I trembled without control. Finally, I felt my mind calm down for a moment. And I took an internal journey, reflecting on the moments of my existence. I felt that my soul and my spirit detached from my body. Slowly they joined that hand that for a moment touched me. My senses remained part of my body, my mind, and my soul. Perceiving this way, time and space accompanied by a strange force penetrated my being. I never ceased to feel how I touched the ground with my feet, to smell the scent of roses, to see the hands of God, and to hear that Voice of God that caused me joy.

Once again, the voice of the one who was sitting on the throne, boomed in my eardrums saying, "Come here my son and sit by my side. I will show you the mysteries of my Kingdom. And I will reveal to you my name, which you will write with symbols and you will make a golden staff rod in the form of my name. I will take you to the confines of space, where no man has walked. And when you finish witnessing all my mysteries, your spirit will become a star. And you will be the Savior of many souls, and you will pass to eternal life in my company. Because I am the creator of all that is visible and invisible. I am the God of Abraham, Jacob, and Isaac, Amen. "

And so it happened, God took me to those mysterious places, and he showed me a book with five chapters, which were written with sacred symbols, and those books describe the principles of his kingdom. After a quick trip for his gardens and its golden streets, he told me, "For the moment you will return to the physical world because it is not your time to die." After He told me those words, He touched my head with a rod, and I instantly felt my spirit return to my body. The Angel accompanied me back through the tunnel of light.

When we finally left that tunnel, which took us about 8 minutes and 6 seconds, The Angel guided me through the desert. We walk among many bushes. When we arrived at a populated area, the Angel said goodbye to me. He put in my hands a purple briefcase.

Inside the briefcase, there was a book and a rock with strange figures. The book was similar to the one shown to me by the one sitting on the throne. In this book that I am putting in your hands today, you will find the answer to all your questions referring to the creation of man and life beyond the afterlife.

After the Angel left, I saw him in the distance as he transformed into pure light. He climbed into the sky slowly and entered a cloud. When I saw the Angel go into the cloud, I tried to open the briefcase that he gave me, but I could not open it. I heard a voice in my mind that said, "It's not the time to open it." An image of the Angel appeared to me in a flash of light. He told me, "Do not worry; you'll have it when God calls the time, and that time will come when you see the third sign in the sky. Three Angels will visit you and talk to you in tongues. And they will take you toward the presence of God.

After the Angel finished talking, I felt better and continued walking among some bushes. When I came out of the bushes, I saw two people walking in my direction, who saw me in anguish and asked, "Are you lost?" I told them, yes and that I was going to Los Angeles, California. They invited me to eat at their house. I accepted the invitation since I was hungry. At that moment, I felt the presence of God. He manifested in the hearts of those people, and that is how the miracles of God happen in my life.

When I entered the house of those people, I felt an inner peace. The first thing they offered me was a glass of water, and then they moved me to the backyard of their house. They sat me on a wooden bench. A little later, they served me a dish of meat with rice and beans, and tortillas. For me, this was a delicacy. I started eating and the lady of the house, asked, "Where are you from?" I gave her my name and place of birth. She told me that it was not right to expose my life. I replied that I would be returning t home to my parents. When I finished eating, I told them that I had to continue on my way, and they accompanied me to the train station.

On the way to the train station, they offered me money for my ticket and $20 dollars extra to buy food. Without thinking twice, I accepted their help, since they did it from the bottom of their heart, also because if I needed it for the road. After buying my ticket, they said goodbye and wished me a happy trip. Shortly after they left, I sat on a bench outside the station. Suddenly, the sky clouded and hail began to rain. It was a terrible downpour. The clerks of the station announced that the train would be delayed because of the rain. The sound of thunder disturbed my nerves, and I felt panicky.

I saw three people dressed in black suits. They were heading toward me. I tried to act normal, but at the same time, I felt very nervous, and I felt my heart beat faster. When they arrived where I was, they spoke to me in a language case unknown to me. They spoke English, and I did not understand anything. The only thing I knew to say in English was "I am an American Citizen." But they talked non-stop and did not understand me.

Coincidentally, a lady got angry and talked to them. I do not know what she said, but minutes later they left without saying anything. The lady explained what was happening; they came for someone. There was a report of an incident in the vicinity. Apparently, people report strange sightings in the sky, but it was not dangerous. I thought that what I experienced was a scare, but when other people saw the event; my vision of light in heaven was real and true. I was surprised to see government agents investigating the sighting of extraterrestrial ships. I did not pay much attention to it since I witnessed everything, talked to an Angel, and saw God sitting on his throne.

I did not say anything to the lady, I thought it was not necessary, but she told me something else, according to her she lied to the agents, telling them that I was her nephew and that I was born here in the United States, but that I live in Mexico. I felt committed to the lady. I do not know what divine power drove her to defend me. But then I thought that she was an Angel sent by God. The Lady told me her name, and I told her mine. She asked, "Why are you traveling alone, and where are you going?" I told her that I had left my house without the consent of my parents and that I ventured off because I wanted to explore the world. The train was approaching the station. They announced it through the loudspeaker. We prepared to board the train, and the lady sat next to me. At those times, I needed company, to talk and to learn a little more of this country. At the same time, I felt safer on the train. She was very kind and invited me to eat. I took some burritos out of her bag. Burrito is a typical Mexican food in the United States. She offered me one and a soft drink.

During the trip, she gave me advice. She told me to try to be a good man. I told her that my longing was to study in this country and then return to Mexico to work and be close to my family. She told me that this would be a wonderful trip full of opportunities, but be aware of drugs, they're readily available. But something that I emphasize many times is, "Never to use drugs because drugs make people sick. They affect society and destroy families. After

36

talking and enjoying the food, I fell into a deep sleep. I slept so comfortably that I did not feel the time pass. When I woke up the lady was no longer by my side, and her bed was empty, I assumed she got off the train and did not tell me. I did not have the opportunity to thank her for her help and the food. I just looked out through the window not having someone to talk to and try to distract my mind. My eyes watched beautiful landscapes created by nature; colorful paintings made by God, I slept a little longer, and the trip was short. I was anxious to reach my destination, to see my friends, and tell them about my adventure.

That was my great longing, but the reality was different, the train was moving at a slow speed, well that's what I felt, but maybe the train ran at its maximum speed. I looked off in the distance and saw something that looked like the lights of a city. The lights were bright, and their radiance accelerated my heart. That emotion consoled me, thinking that my destiny was near. It was the city of Los Angeles, California that was my destiny, and it was only a few kilometers away.

Before arriving at the train station, a vision of my childhood came to my mind. I remembered when I was six years old. On that sunny day, I was sitting in a chair on the patio of my house. And to my right side, I had a table, and on the table, a glass of lemonade, a book, and a notebook. While I finished my homework, I noticed the movement of the sun on the ground as the shadow of a tree moved slowly. After a while, I paid attention to the movement of the branches from the tree, and asked, "What is the invisible force that moves the branches? Is it the same force that moves the planets? At my young age, I could not find the answer in my mind, and I asked several of my professors, but apparently, they also did not know what that strength was. They just told me it was the force of gravity.

I entertained contemplating the path of the sun. I was wondering, "Where was the sun hidden at night? By what supernatural force did it return the next day?" I always picture being on an airplane and following the sun to discover its hiding place, and what it would be like to always live in the light of day. But that is impossible, I know. I also know that it is a mystery for humans why God created our universe, composed of light and darkness. Where the light is attributed to Jesus Christ and darkness to Lucifer. Eliminating each other, every day and night. Also, sometimes I sat in that same chair during the night to see the stars across the sky. Some of the stars captivated me more than others, such as the belt of Orion's Belt and the Ursa Major. Contemplating the sky at night, I asked more questions, and one of those questions is, "Who created the universe? Maybe it was God?

For me, it would be interesting to answer all these questions now that I have a little more knowledge transmitted by God and his Angels. But just like other wise people, my answers will only be my opinion. They would not give a definitive answer to it; everything would be speculation. The philosophical subjects have their disadvantages, and one of them is that there is no absolute, exact, and true answer which can satisfy the primitive mind of man. Well, returning to my train, I am approaching the city of Los Angeles. This moment is what I was longing for; I could not contain my happiness, and my eyes shed a few tears.

When I get off the bus, I kneel down, kissed the ground, raise my arms, and look up to heaven to thank God. I could not contain my crying, and for a moment, I forgot that I still had to get to my destination, the city of Pasadena. Again, I entrusted myself to God so that he would guide me and protect me. In this city, it was easy to get lost as it was a place unknown to me. And the ironic thing was that I did not speak the English language, and did he know how to communicate with people. I had the hope of finding people who spoke in Spanish, and in that way, I could communicate with them. For the time being, I had confidence in myself, and I was determined to reach my destination. In spite of everything, I was already in the United States, the only thing that afflicted me was the

38

following; In my journey I lost my agenda, in which I wrote the addresses and phone numbers of my friends, I only remembered the location of the house, which was between Orange Grove and Faire Oaks streets.

Chapter Four

My arrival in Los Angeles California.

Finally arriving in Los Angeles, I left the train station and began to wander in the night, and I was alone, in a vast city and without speaking the English language. At first, I felt fear, but as I walked through the streets, I was armed with courage and determination, which was greater than my fears. I knew God would give me the strength to arrive alive to my destiny. I saw two people walking down the desolate street; they went in my direction and asked about the Mission of Los Angeles, California. They stopped for a moment and kindly told me how to get to my destination. I walked through several streets and some alleys full of people, and then I saw a sea of people in tents, drinking alcohol and smoking drugs, fear began to take over. I left the alleys and walked along the central streets, in the distance I saw a group of people in line to enter a building.

I made my way to that building and noticed that a man was upset. I spoke kindly to him and got into the slow moving line. When it was my turn to enter the Mission, I felt great relief in my heart. Finally, they ordered me to come in, take a tray, a plate and a spoon. I continued on the line, and when I got to the kitchen, ordered a sandwich, oatmeal, and some fruit. Everything was delicious, for me it was like a delicacy from God. At the end of dinner, I asked; "Are beds available to spend the night here?" They told me that there were no longer any beds available for that night. With no other choice, I had to sleep on the street.

When leaving the Mission, I walked among the dark alleys to find a safe place to spend the night. I found some cardboard from a trash can and used some newspapers to shelter me. When I laid down on the cardboard, the happy days I lived with my family came to my mind. I wondered at that moment, "Had I decided to leave my house and live like a beggar?" I could not find a logical answer to my question. What I did know beforehand, that something had driven me out of my house and that was not the time to repent; on the contrary try to be brave, and face the consequences of my actions. Although I try to be strong all the time, there were moments in which, I could not contain my emotions. And more than once, I shed a couple of tears.

That night I tried to sleep peacefully, to get up early and wake up with courage. Inwardly I knew, that my journey was not easy and that I would continue to find obstacles in my way. In my prayers, I asked God for forgiveness, for all my sins, and I thanked him for keeping me alive on my journey. When I finished praying, before falling asleep, I look up at the sky, and I thought I heard a low voice. I tried to sleep, but I could not do it since the noise of the cars was very loud.

There were moments when I closed my eyes and imagined that I was lying in a beautiful and safe place. But when I opened them again I was still in this harsh reality; I was in the same place; lying on the ground sheltered by newspapers. The night became eternal waiting for the dawn, to be able to walk by day in the city and look for the buses to Pasadena. I got up at five o'clock in the morning in that alley, although I could not sleep all night, was glad to see the sunlight. Without any other remedy, I got up off the ground, and I prepared to go to the Mission to have breakfast.

I hurried to be among the first in the line, but when I reached the doors, I saw a sea of people awaiting their turn. Finally, I went in and took a tray, poured me a cup of coffee and made some bread and butter. With the food in my hands, I prepared to sit down at a table, and suddenly a couple of African Americans sat together. But when trying to connect with them, I realized that they did not speak

41

Spanish. I did not know what they were saying between them, but they laughed out loud, and I thought they were telling each other jokes. I played dumb. When I finished my breakfast, I said thanks to the cooks and the guards.

When I left the Mission, I did not know what direction to take. So I decided to look for a park and ask people how to get to Pasadena. I thought that was the right thing to do, I walked between the streets, but I did not find any parks, what I saw were groups of people, sitting on benches, waiting for public transport. I greeted them and asked them, "Do you know where Pasadena is?" They answered yes, and they told me which street to take the bus. I headed towards Main Street, and upon arriving, I saw some buses parked. I ran and asked a man again, and he kindly told me, which was the correct bus to take.

I was overjoyed to have found the bus! However, the next problem; I didn't have money to pay my fare, so, shamefully, I asked for money in the streets. All that, I did out of necessity; the only thing I needed was a little bit of money to buy the ticket. A man offered to buy my bus ticket, and said, "Help for you today, and tomorrow for me; you never know when you need others." I thanked him for his kindness; we sat on a bench, to talk while we waited on the bus. He had told me that he was already living in the United States for about 30 years. I admired him and asked him about his family, but he did not answer my question. When he saw the bus approaching, he ordered me to get on first, since he would pay my fare. We sat together and continued talking, and I learned more about this country.

The trip took 40 minutes or more, and when we entered the city of Pasadena, the man told me where to get off. He pointed out the indicated street through the window; here is the intersection of Orange Grove and Fair Oaks streets. At last, I felt a great relief inside me; now my dream will be a reality. Thank God I arrived at my destination, but I remembered that I did not have the exact address since I had lost my agenda on the way. I decided to walk towards the west of the city, at the end of the day it finished in front of the Pasadena Rose Bowl. I was disoriented and considered I may have been walking in the opposite direction, but that did not matter to me at the time, because I was already in Pasadena. For a moment I cleared my mind and contemplated the Rose Bowl stadium. I took things slowly and relaxed on the grass, closed my eyes and thanked God.

Fatigue overcame me, and I fell into a deep sleep, I didn't notice that time had passed by, and when I woke up, it was completely dark. I loaded my backpack on. And I roamed around feeling lost. I just wanted to leave that place. I took the main street that went under a bridge, I went up, and I walked along the bridge, and for a moment I felt free and safe. Also came thoughts of my childhood, remembering those days when I walked on the arches of my town. After contemplating that part of the city, I got off the bridge and began to search for a place to sleep, fortunately among some bushes; I found a mat, which served useful as a bed. I spread the mat on the ground and laid down on it, closed my eyes and asked myself, "What would my parents think of me? What would be their reaction if they saw me in this condition?"

That night, sleep found me and I slept like a little angel, I woke up at six in the morning. The first thing I heard was the singing of the birds and the sound of water running over a stream. After thanking God, I began my journey again, and to my surprise on the main street, I saw a street sign that said, "Orange Grove." I then realized I had not gone away from the destination I was looking for after all. I went to the east side of the city on Orange Grove Avenue and arrived at a gas station on Fair Oaks Street. And suddenly I saw a group of people walking on the sidewalk. I felt panic because they were in black suits, they looked like the inspectors I saw at the train station. One of them spoke to me and asked, "Good morning, I wonder if you have a minute to talk a little?" I replied, yes.

He invited me to have a coffee, I accepted the invitation, and we headed to a restaurant with Mexican food. We arrived at the restaurant, ordered our coffee and sat at a table. After a while of talking, they told me that they belong to a Church by name; "Jehovah's Witnesses." One of them asked me if I believed in God? I immediately answered, "Of course! I believe in the one true God. And as proof of my faith here I carry a bible with me, and let me tell you; that I had an encounter with God in the desert." My response was not to their liking, and they laughed at me. I allowed them to evangelize me since I felt a need to hear the good news, to listen to them I felt tranquility in my heart. They spoke to me of an earthly Kingdom of God, which I did not understand, since I had not read my Bible. Before saying goodbye, they said, "Jehovah loves you and takes care of you. Follow your path and never give up." Finally, they said goodbye and gave me their names along with their phone numbers, in case I needed something in the future.

I left the restaurant and headed to Fair Oaks Street, and arrived at the intersection of Villa Street. There I saw a group of people, talking among themselves. I interrupted their talk and asked, "What are you doing standing here?" One of them answered, "We are day laborers, and we are waiting for work." I did not understand what that person told me, but I stayed there talking to him. And out of nowhere a car pulled up in front of us, and the driver of the vehicle offered us work. The new friend and I got into the car, and he took us to a car wash to detail his cars. During the workday, I asked various questions to my new friend, one of the questions was as follows; "Do you know any laborers from the city of Mexico City?", and he responded "I certainly do, and some of the laborers congregate in Villa Park."

When we returned from work, I asked him to tell me how to get to Villa Park, he decided to accompany me, since he slept in the streets and parks, and that night he was going to sleep in the Villa Park. I accepted his help, and we headed towards the park; but before arriving at the park, we bought a roasted chicken, sodas and tortillas. We came to the park and started eating, after about 30 minutes, to my surprise two of my friends Miguel and Javier happened to arrive. They did not expect to see me in that place, I greeted them, and afterward, we talked a little. Miguel asked me, "How did you make the trip alone?" I told him part of my story and of my experience in the desert. I invited them to eat roasted chicken, after eating they asked me to come to their house. When we arrived at his home, I was surprised to see many unknown people. There were more than 25 people there, some were passing through and others were waiting for their relatives come to get them.

I felt calm and at peace knowing I had a safe place to sleep. As the days passed, I realized; how the system of life here in the United States operates. Work to earn money. Pay monthly rent, until you die. Where in Mexico, you cannot ask more than asking for life. Here, I could continue working as a day laborer in Villa Street, I remember the method I used, to get the attention of the employers, I pretended to speak in English when I did not know much about the language. The days I did not work, reflected in my situation, and I understood that without an education, life would not be as comfortable here. I always thought about studying and elevating myself. I wanted to live a better life and take advantage of the thousands of opportunities that this country offers. Although sometimes I didn't earn much, even to eat, that did not discourage me because I was still on the warpath.

There were so many days that I did not work, especially on rainy days, and those days I ended up eating at the Pasadena Mission, after eating I would search of work, I visited restaurants, workshops, and many more businesses, until I finally got a job in a warehouse, with that small salary I managed to rent my apartment. With my job and my apartment, the next thing I did was to enroll in high school. My ambition was to learn English and thus be able to study at the University. My goal was to study Mathematics,

Molecular Biology or Astrophysics, those three branches of natural science called my attention. Then months and years passed, I could not finish the 12th grade of high school since my work was a bit unstable. Sometimes I would return to Mexico to visit my family. So I went for a few years, up and down and my last time I entered to the United States was in the year 1990.

Birth of my daughter, Brandy.

Time passed, and in 1995 I met a beautiful young woman named Yenny. We became close friends and with the passage of time, we decided to live together as a couple, and then to marry. After seven months of our relationship, she got pregnant, which caused us a lot of happiness. We both enjoyed the pregnancy as a couple. I always accompanied her to the prenatal appointments. When they performed the first ultrasound, I became filled with joy when I saw on the screen the figure of a little baby girl, inside the belly of the woman that I loved. I dreamed of seeing my baby in my arms, taking care of her and giving her all my love as a father. Unfortunately, they informed us that our baby girl ran a high risk of being born with certain health problems. That news devastated us when listening to it, I looked my wife in the eyes and hugged her tightly, I kissed her on the forehead, and I also gave her words of encouragement.

To add more pain to our suffering, they suggested that it was preferable for her to abort. I did not answer anything; we asked them for a moment to be alone. Being alone in the room, I asked my wife, "What do you want to do?" She answered without thinking twice, "I want to have this baby girl no matter what happens, even if I sacrifice my life for her; I want you to be a father." I had never seen my wife so determined in something, she showed me at that moment that she would be a great mother. After a little while, I saw

46

her with tears in her eyes, and she said, "I do not think our baby girl has health problems." I did not say anything, I just listen to her, and I understood that she wanted to continue with the pregnancy. Finally, I told her, I am on your side to support you in everything. We both understood that only God knew why this happened to us.

When I finished the conversation with my wife, I called the nurses and told them that it was a decision. They just shook their heads and told us that the pregnancy was high risk. We did not answer anything and we left the clinic, after leaving the clinic, I took my wife to eat a hamburger, we went to our favorite restaurant, Johnny Rockets. While we were eating, my wife and I began to reminisce about how we met and began talking about the first dance we danced and the first kiss. Those memories made us laugh so much that we forgot our anguish - for a few minutes. But, thoughts of our situation came again, our reality was stronger than fiction and we could not ignore our situation.

We stared into each other's eyes and at the same time, we both wondered if that was a punishment from God? In order to calm my wife down as she became emotional, I took her by the hand, and we got up from the table. We left the restaurant to buy her ice cream, and we walked along the Colorado Boulevard. We got to the City Hall; we went through the corridors and sat on a bench. That place gave us peace of mind that we did not want to go home. As if something supernatural comforted us. We contemplated that place, I went and cut a rose and gave it to her with a kiss. I told her that I loved her a lot. She smiled and hugged me tightly, she said do not let me go, please. I squeezed her in my arms and shed a couple of tears.

It was already dusk and the sun was hidden, I told her that I could see the moon and the brightest star of all. She told me that if she died giving birth, her spirit would be in that star, and that from above would take care of our daughter and me. I did not know what to say and I suggested that we should go to her parents'

47

house. She wanted to see her mother and her dad, to give them the bad news. Upon entering the house we saw that her mother was cooking chicken soup. But seeing our faces, she wondered, "Why so sad?" She said, "What's going on with my children!?" My wife cried and ran to hug her mother. With a lump in her throat, she tried to explain the results of her pregnancy, telling her that her pregnancy was high risk. And that possibly she or the baby could die in childbirth. For a moment we all fell silent, we looked at each other and my mother-in-law said, "Don't always believe in the doctor's end results, they're often wrong and can make mistakes."

We thought the same thing, I answered her, now it's just about waiting and taking care of my wife's health, I told them. My mother-in-law couldn't control herself; she and I began to cry next to my wife, I knew that this news was difficult for the whole family. I think that life sometimes hits us hard to prove how strong our faith is in God. The months went by and my wife continued with her pregnancy, and I continued to be supportive of her. I remember that during that time I had two jobs, to cover the expenses of our home and bills. The days passed and the seventh month of her pregnancy arrived, one night she felt labor pains. She called me at work and I asked permission to leave early.

I was happy to hear the news of my wife, but I also felt bad, because of the risk of her pregnancy. I told her that I would be home in 45 minutes, before hanging up, I suggested that she notify her parents. I went straight from my supervisor, to ask permission to leave early. Thankfully my supervisor was understanding and without further questions, he authorized me to leave early. I headed towards the parking lot, and one of my coworkers asked me why I was leaving in such a big hurry? I told him that my wife was about to give birth. I said goodbye to him and got into my car, I felt my feet trembling. Maybe it was the emotions or desperation.

The thrill of being a father invaded me and as I drove, I imagined myself with my little girl in my arms, cooing and talking with her. I also saw in my mind a vision of my daughter on her fifteenth birthday, celebrating her birth. And next I visualized her wedding, marrying in a white dress, and I was surrendering my daughter to her husband in front of the altar of the Virgin of Guadalupe. I wanted to fly over the cars to get home quickly and help my wife prepare to go to the hospital. The road seemed long, but I managed as fast as I could. I drove there in 30 minutes. When I walked in the door of my apartment, I saw my wife lying on the bed; she had towels wrapped around her body. "What's wrong, are you okay?" I asked. She told me that her water broke.

I packed a few things in a backpack, necessary for the birth of our baby. I took my wife by the hand and helped her out of bed; I put on her shoes and walked slowly towards the car. I felt desperate to help her, as she was harrowing with complaints of pain, I tried to calm her with my words of encouragement, but even that did not reassure her. The road to the Hospital was an eternal nightmare since all the stop lights we came to were red. It seemed almost as if someone was intentionally changing the light to red. When we finally arrived at the hospital, we entered the Emergency room, registered her and they attended her almost immediately. As soon as they admitted her, they assigned her a room, where she was alone and I went out to look for a public telephone, to give notice to her family about their daughter's situation. When her mother answered the phone, she heard my shaky voice and asked. Is everything ok with my daughter?" I told her that everything was fine and that her daughter was about to give birth at the hospital and I also gave her the room number, she told me that she would arrive in 20 minutes.

Back in the room, I saw my wife crying because she did not know what would happen to our baby. A group of doctors and nurses were taking care of her. My wife told them that her pregnancy was very risky. After they examined her and reviewed her prenatal history, they recommended that the birth to be performed by Caesarean Section. The nurses took my wife to a different room. I did not separate myself for a moment from her side, I felt light-headed, and like a zombie, I did not know if I was happy, sad, scared or worried, or all of it at the same time; I could not contain my crying. Two hours later, they were preparing her for Caesarian, of course by then her relatives were already in the waiting room; her mother asked to be present, the doctors authorized her to enter the surgery room. I was always attentive to the entire medical procedure, I wanted to see my baby born, and when the moment came that she was born, I cut the cord, and they allowed me to hold her for a moment.

This was the moment I waited anxiously, and I enjoyed it to the fullest. My eyes were filled with tears of joy when I held my little girl in my arms, I looked into her eyes and I kissed her on the forehead, she smiled and looked at me with a lot of affection. I called her by her name and smiled. I looked back to see my wife, and she extended her arms to hold our daughter. I placed our beautiful baby girl on her chest and she looked at her with much tenderness and caressed her with great delicacy. I can never forget that image of my wife, holding her daughter for the first time. Amazing maternal love in all its splendor. Slowly I approached my wife and embraced my two Loves, my baby girl was rolling her eyes around trying to recognize my voice. I lost the notion of time when contemplating my daughter, I did not want to let go. I did not want to stop seeing her adorable face. After a while, they told us that they had to take my Bebita to bathe her and dress her. I gave them the clothes that my wife brought for her.

The nurses placed Brandy on a special baby carrier, and they brought her to bathe her. Suddenly nurses shouted cries causing alarm, they shouted "Not breathing" and quickly took me out of the room, and told me to wait in the lobby area. On my way out of the room, I saw a team of nurses and doctors arrive. I did not know what was happening with my girl, as I tried to calm down and

50

walked at the end of the corridor. They spent more than ten minutes and did not tell me anything about the state of my baby Brandy. I headed towards the waiting room, where my brother and my in-laws were. Upon seeing me enter, my brother asked me. "Is everything okay?" I told him that I did not know anything about Brandy's state of health, that they had taken me out of the room, due to a health issue. I closed my eyes and told my brother, how unfair life has been for me. I'm just living a few moments of happiness, enjoying the joy of being a father for the first time. And in the blink of an eye, everything changes. I could not contain my crying, one of the Nurses came out and told us that we could go in to see the girl.

I asked, "What is my daughter's condition?" She answered by saying, "In a moment we will explain what is the condition of the baby is." I went in and saw my little girl in a hospital crib with a tube in her mouth, several things attached to her legs; and many items connected to her little heart. I made myself caress her. One of the Doctors explained to me that Brandy could not breathe on her own and that her condition was critical. My heart was torn to see my girl suffering, slowly I approached her and took her hand, at the same time I gently stroked her head and called her by her name, "Brandy, how are you my baby?" and she turned to see me and in her eyes showed her pain. I asked God why, because he sent me such strong proofs that everything would be okay. In times like these, you do not know how to react or what to say, the voice goes out and words are missing, to express human pain. Only with my body parts, the nurses noticed my pain and consoled me by giving me a hug and saying that they felt for us.

I did not hear any response from God, my being was devastated when I saw my baby in that condition, I called one of the Nurses and told her that I wanted to hold my daughter, two of them came and they helped to get her to my arms. When I felt her body so delicate in my hands, my paternal instinct woke up, embrace her

51

delicately. When I held her in my arms, I kept contemplating her beautiful eyes and her face; I gave her a kiss on her cheeks. I could not accept my daughter's medical condition, I thought it was just a bad dream; one of those dreams that upon awakening are quickly forgotten. My wife wanted to see her daughter and the nurses helped me carry her to her bed. She also deserved to admire and caress her baby girl my wife was surprised to see Brandy connected to so many machines. Suddenly Yenny was overcome with emotion and started screaming out of desperation, "It's not fair! It's not fair!" The nurses had to sedate my wife.

While my wife was being handled by the Nurses, one of the nurses asked me to leave the room for a moment. I did not want to leave my daughter and my wife alone, I felt that my obligation as a husband and father was to be there with them. Seeing that my wife could not calm down, they administered another sedative. To calm my own anxiety, I decided to go for a walk in the parking lot, look for my car to smoke a cigarette. When I got in my car and turned on the ignition, ironically at the radio station was playing one of my favorite songs ("My Angel"). I lit my cigarette with a match and I took my cup of coffee I closed my eyes and reclined my head on the seat, opened the sunroof to the car and contemplated the moon and the stars. I felt alone like never before, and when the song finished I returned to my wife's room.

When I opened the door to the lobby I headed between the corridors, towards the maternity ward. Before arriving in the waiting room, I felt a great need to pray, and continued walking to the end of the hall. I huddled in a corner and cried out the name of God, I asked Him to acknowledge my prayers. I did not want to see my daughter and my wife suffer. Lend my hands to heaven, and I beseech God to hear my prayers. "Do not take my daughter, she is part of my life and my being. I beg of you to take my life, my spirit, and my body instead."

Suddenly I felt that my whole body become faint, and I could not get off the floor. I continued praying without control, I felt the spirit of God had taken possession of me. After a while of praying, I heard behind me a soft captivating voice from a woman. I turned quickly to see who it was, and indeed it was a woman, who approached me. She was in a white robe and a purple veil covered her face. On her head, she wore a golden diadem, with seven symbols. The noise of her sandals was coming more and more close to me. Finally, being next to me, she touched my shoulders and called me by my name. She said, "Jesús, what is it that afflicts you, my son? What is your pain about?" I replied, "My newborn daughter is being devastated, between life and death. And God has not heard my prayers, I do not know what to do anymore; I would like to have the divine power to heal her."

She responded to my comment, "Do not worry anymore, my son, that's why I'm here to comfort you."God sent me to be your helper, but before giving you His message; take my hands, and close your eyes, and listen carefully to what I am going to tell you. God is not mad with you, nor with your wife. He knows what He does and why He does it. And nobody can question His actions, remember that He is the supreme creator of all things. Only you humans do not understand His mysteries. He knows perfectly well what you are going through, and He will not allow more suffering in your heart. Get up and go with your wife and your daughter, take these two Rosaries, which I have elaborated with my hands, one is rose pink and the other is black. Go and place the rose pink one on your daughter's neck and the black one on your wife's' neck. That it's the message of God, to give you two Rosaries which contain the answer to your afflictions." After giving me the Rosaries she hugged me and left.

I ran to my wife's room and told her I saw a woman who looked like the Virgin Mary. She gave me two Rosaries one is for you and the other is for Brandy, I put the Rosary around her neck, and I kissed it. A moment later my wife asked to see our daughter. I told her that it was impossible for the Doctors to authorize us to see her. I went to ask the Nurses at the Nurse station about the condition of my daughter, one of the Nurses allowed me to see her from afar. She allowed me to look at her and I saw her sad face, she could not breathe, her eyes were full of tears and her face was scrunching up every time she tried to take a breath. You could tell she had a lot of pain in her tiny body. I never imagined that I would live to see something so exasperating. When one plans to have a family, one only visualizes the most beautiful things in life, to see the children grow up healthy and happy.

After looking at my daughter, one of the nurses called me and told me that the doctors wanted to talk to me. Enter the room and when the doctors arrived, they told us that our daughter's condition was more delicate. Since her organs were exposed, to correct the issue they would have to do multiple surgeries. At the end of the conversation, they told us that it was better for the girl to leave. Only then would she be free from suffering. But when we heard that, my wife exclaimed, "It is not true what they say!" I held her hand tight and with tears in my eyes, I told her to calm down. I asked for a moment alone with my wife, the doctors left the room and I talked to my wife, but she did not pay attention to my words. Her pale face said more than a thousand words, finally, I managed to calm her down, and then told me that she would rather die. Those strong words cut to the deepest part of my heart.

We were both feeling depressed, and we did not know what to do. Then suddenly the woman who gave me the Rosaries appeared to us both and told us, "God's plan is perfect, He will never fail you." Everything you are living now is very painful, I know, but you have to resign yourself to the will of God." She hugged us and kissed us on the forehead, finally gave me a paper with four symbols on it, and left the room. As she walked away she paused and said, "Take care of your wife because when she heals, she will give you a son." Then it was when I was assured, that it was a sign from God. We reassured ourselves for a moment and looking at our girl from afar we decided that Brandy should leave earth to relieve her pain. We both knew beforehand, that this decision was not easy, because we were not prepared for all this. But we entrust the soul of our daughter to God. I kissed my wife and told her I loved her. She smiled and told me to call the Nurses.

Without further thought, I went in search of the Nurses, informing them that we had made our decision. They came to the room, and my wife told them with a very low tone of voice, "We'll let Brandy leave us" As soon as she had comprehended what she was talking about, she was in shock and suddenly she lost consciousness. They told me to give my wife a moment to recover from the shock. I sat in a chair and meditated a few minutes when I closed my eyes I fell into a deep sleep, I did not know how long I slept, but when I woke up my wife already felt better. The hardest thing was yet to come, I felt the desire to spend more time with my baby; but it was impossible to avoid it, the clock on the wall was ticking, and the moment arrived when they told us, it is time to say goodbye to your child. They dressed her in clothes, which my wife had bought before she was born.

The Doctors gave us the opportunity to say goodbye to our daughter, and they brought her to my wife's room. When they arrived with her, they recommended that we take her with care. My wife took her in her arms and placed her on her chest.

While I was looking closely at the movements of my daughter, I could not hold back my tears; I knew that these were the last minutes of my little Brandy's life. We embraced our baby together, we tried to enjoy that moment at its best. We sang those songs that my wife listened to at home when she was pregnant. And Brandy opened her eyes and smiled as if responding to our voices.

These were the saddest moments of my life. I felt my whole being was extinguished. After twenty minutes of having her in my arms, I did not want to let her go. But the Doctors became angry at how long we were taking to say goodbye and told me that it was time to disconnect her from the breathing devices. I wanted to be with my girl, until her last moment of life. I knew that when I heard her last breath, it would be as if I died with her. I begged the Doctors to let me be with her. Finally, they agreed to let me stay with my daughter, and hold her by the hand. At the same time, I watched them disconnect the machines from her body. I approached a little closer and I gave her a kiss on her forehead, shortly after she was disconnected I kissed her forehead, and she opened her eyes and stared at me.

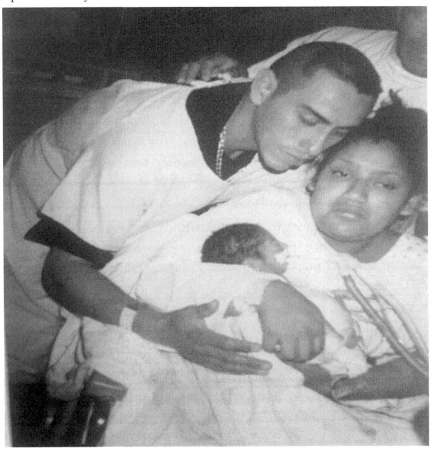

At Pasadena Huntington Hospital; Brandy, Jenny and I

I heard a noise a couple of times, as her breathing was sharper, every time the air entered her lungs. She took squeezed my thumb on my right hand and clung to it very strongly, it seemed that she sensed her departure. I contemplated the color of her eyes, they were a bright clear coffee color. I spoke to her with a lot of love, and with a soft voice told her that everything would be fine. And she reacted to my words as if she understood. And she moved her head as if saying "no, no" her movements caused me to feel the deepest amount of compassion for her suffering, I kept repeating her name, "Brandy, Brandy" and she turned to see me with tears in her eyes. After a while, one of the doctors approached and explained that they had to inject morphine.

The Doctor injected her with morphine so that she would stop suffering, and when injecting it I felt that my soul left my body. I loved my girl, and she was leaving. I returned my hand to hers and she grasped my index finger. Her lungs struggled to breathe and little by little her heart stopped beating, she did not release my index finger, I could not contain my cries in thinking that my Brandy was fading. I prayed for my Baby so that God may receive her in His Kingdom. At that time, my faith was greater than ever. And that faith in God was what kept me on my feet, all those hours of anguish. The doctors returned to observe Brandy's condition, and they administered a second dose of morphine. Again, I felt that my spirit was leaving my body, seeing how morphine was flowing through my daughter's veins. The helplessness of not being able to help my daughter caused me immobility in my body, and I felt the fury of this reality. But it was so surreal, that it almost didn't feel like we were on the earth at that moment of time. The only thing I could do was to observe her, caress her and speak to her tenderly, speaking her name. She just looked at me in pain or... fear.

After more than thirty minutes my baby girl was barely breathing, the doctors told me that my girl did not die because I was there talking to her. They almost pushed me out of the room, because I did not want to let go of my girl. The doctors and Nurses forced me to leave. And when I finally let her go, my girl stopped breathing and I heard her last breath. Turn my gaze to the sky, as if to see the spirit of my daughter leave. I asked God to receive her in His Kingdom since she was one more soul in His celestial choir. There is no greater suffering than seeing your child slip into eternity; there are no words to describe my pain. I got up off the floor and returned to my wife's room with my heart devastated.

On my way to the room, my wife asked me for Brandy. I told her that she had already left and that she was in a better place. The minutes continued and we could not contain our tears. My wife and I wanted to have our child in our arms, to make caresses and call her by name. I did not know what else to tell my wife, just hug her to comfort her and give her my security. Now came the hardest thing for me, to have to say goodbye to my daughter. Nobody in the world could ever prepare you for these moments. There are no manual instructions that prepare us for these painful moments; only faith in God strengthened us to accept the loss of our daughter.

Now, the next thing to do was to say our last goodbye to my baby girl, and arrange her funeral. I asked my friend Gaby and her sister Teresa, to help me. With their help everything was easier for us since my wife was still recovering in the hospital. Gaby suggested that I go to the same funeral home where she offered a service to her own daughter Konie. My friend was so kind as to accompany me to the funeral home. I paid for the services of the funeral and cemetery, now only the transfer of Brandy.

Two days after the service was reserved, the funeral home received Brandy's tiny body, and they told me that they already had her in their possession. The service was scheduled for August 08, 1996. On the day of the service, I went to the funeral home, in the company of my two friends Gaby and Teresa; together we dressed Brandy for her funeral service.

We entered the room where my daughter laid, and I took her in my hands. With great delicacy we began to dress her, I had bought her a white dress, with a bow, leotards and little shoes. We put a rosary on around her neck and a candle in her right hand. When I saw her dressed in white, I could not stop the crying and I kissed her little mouth.

I caressed her and talked to her, imagining that she could hear me and understand me, but her body did not move. Gaby told me that she could not listen to me, that she wanted me to be in reality. But, I did not stop talking to my daughter. I thought that if she listened to me and that maybe she would open her eyes again. From one moment to another I felt faint; I did not know what to do when seeing my daughter's lifeless body. My mind was transported to another dimension, in that unknown dimension in which, only the spirit can enter.

At Pasadena California; Saying goodbye to my daughter, Brandy

When we finished dressing her I contemplated her for a moment, I closed my eyes and visualized her in the sky as if she were an Angel. And when I opened my eyes, it was so painful; it was time to put her in her coffin. And again, I did not want to separate from my daughter forever. I wasn't ready to let go. But I understood that it was impossible to stop the time, and it arrived at that moment when my hands released her little body inside the coffin.

My daughter's face will never be erased from my mind, I know it's hard to understand but - that's life. Nobody tells us how to overcome the loss of a loved one. Nobody has a written formula, or a miracle pill to heal from that kind of pain. Only time helps to heal this type of wound. As the hours passed, my friends and my wife's relatives arrived at the funeral home. They all gave me compassion and kind words. I thanked them for their support and for their company during those difficult times. After a Mass performed by a priest, we prepared to take Brandy's body to the cemetery. As I lifted her small coffin to the car, I felt my heart tear and bleed internally. It was so deep I knew the scar would never heal.

The driver of the vehicle left the parking lot, in the direction of the cemetery. With tears on my face I followed the car; my mind was still out of reality. I drove by the power of the Holy Spirit, the Divine power of God kept me alert. I looked in the mirror and saw all the vehicles of my friends, following my car, it formed a caravan. After driving for more than thirty minutes on the streets of Pasadena and San Gabriel. At last, we reached our destination, the Resurrection Cemetery. I parked and got out of the car, ran like a desperate crazy man to unload my baby girl for her event.

I ached to feel her in my arms once more, and now my time with her would be for the very last time.

Carefully we lowered the coffin of my Brandy, but before she was placed into the pit, she was placed on a table to give her one last goodbye. I sang two songs that are very popular in Mexico, "Las

Golondrinas and Amor Eterno." It's the song by which Mexicans say goodbye. I knelt in front of the table they placed her on and laid my head against it. I spoke to her in silence, "My daughter" I told her next, "I promise that I will never forget my dear child, you are an Angel of God who brought joy to our lives. Just to remember the day your mommy broke the news that she was pregnant. That day was the happiest of my life, those few months of joy, and now with all the pain inside me, I say goodbye." I sobbed, "I love you my Bebita, today you take a part of my being, and my heart breaks into two pieces upon your departure." After talking to her, I got up and took a few steps back. And I gave the opportunity to all those who accompanied me, to say a few words to Brandy and say goodbye to her. Then, it was time to put the coffin in the grave. Take a fist of the earth in my right hand, and throw it on the coffin, saying so; "Dust you are and dust you will become". And all the people present did the same, a few hours later I was left alone. I tried to calm down before returning home.

Finally, I took a few flowers from my daughter's grave. When I got home I gave the flowers to my wife, and she let go in a sea of tears. I hugged her very tight, and I told her that our daughter was already with God. That day without a doubt was one of the saddest days of my life, but I understood that life goes on, and that time will help me to heal that journey.

Time went by and my wife and I regained our strength. And so it was after a year my wife got pregnant again. And there was born a sweet baby named Jesse, he brought happiness to our lives. Until today, I understand through my son Jesse, the pain my father had when I left my home in Mexico.

Chapter Five

My Second Encounter with God in Pasadena California.

Over the next year, Yenny and I had started having problems in our relationship. And in only one year after the birth of my son Jesse, my wife and I separated from each other. Now there would be another challenge in my life. The most difficult for me was to accept my reality. At first, I did not understand why this happened to me, and I came to think that it was a punishment from God. But with the passage of time, I matured and managed to understand that everything was over between us. I cannot deny that when I saw her leave my eyes were filled with tears, especially when I remembered all the moments we lived through together; But, I tried to be strong, and I said goodbye to her like a gentleman. I hugged her and kissed her on the forehead, I looked her in the eyes and told her that when she needed my support, I would be there to help her, I would do it for her and my daughter Brandy R.I.P, and my son Jesse.

I thought about how difficult it would be for my son to grow up without his father, but there were no more chances. Our decision to separate was firm on both sides. I felt that nothing in the world could console me. I had to resign myself to this situation. My ex-wife had already found love with another person. As a human I felt an uncontrollable rage boiling inside me, but I maintained calm in order to not cause any more problems. I asked God for wisdom and understanding, to dictate the reasons for this separation. I'm not going to lie. I spent many nights thinking about what failure as a husband I was. Looking back, I realize that it was my immaturity at that time in my life. I admit that I did not give them a millionaire's life, but humbly I learned to provide the essential things for the home. I remember that I had two jobs and at the same time I attended College. Because I was not home for much of the time, she felt I did not dedicate the necessary time for our relationship.

There were moments that I could not assimilate, what was happening in our lives. I remember that before we lived together, we both talked about our plans for the future. She dreamed to be a Doctor one day. I wanted to be a Professor of Mathematics. Life didn't deliver us what we had expected from it. I do not know how she changed so suddenly. I saw our home crumble like a sandcastle, and again I felt like it was a punishment from God. Failure after failure came to us. Every time I started something new, obstacles and challenges appeared in my way. All of these life challenges caused my dreams to vanish from my hands. Finally, Yenny and I parted for good, and we shared custody of Jesse. We had to go to court to get things finalized, and to Yenny's surprise, the decision of the Judge for joint custody was 80% custody for Yenny and 20% for me. She thought as the mother, she would get 100% custody, but the judge saw it differently. I could only see my son on weekends. For me, it was a good decision on the part of the Judge, because I wanted to stop fighting with my ex on the maintenance. With a reasonable monthly payment of support and two days of visitation, I agreed this was good. I gave God grace for being fair and generous with me. I waited anxiously on weekends to see and enjoy the presence of my son.

However, I quickly learned that two days were not enough, for a father who loved his child so much. But history had already been written that way, and I would have to fight for the love of my son. The separation of my wife and the custody of my son were not the only problems that overwhelmed me in those days. A few months before going to court, I suffered a car accident; in which I almost lost my life. I did not know what was more painful, not having my son, or the physical pain caused by the car accident, or maybe it was a combination of the two discomforts. My memories of these hard times remain with me. But by the grace of God, I made it through.

The car accident happened in the mountains of San Bernardino, during my working hours. I used to work as a driver for an automobile company, located in the city of Cerritos California. I remember the day of my accident; I have it in my mind as if it happened yesterday. That day was a typical day like any other, and I woke up early as always to go to school, before arriving at school I stopped to have breakfast at an American food restaurant.

After eating my breakfast, I went to the school to attend my classes. I saw that the hours passed very slowly, I felt like the time stopped. The minutes were dragging on. At last, I left my classes and headed towards my work, after driving between the traffic for more than thirty minutes, I arrived at my job, and I reported to my supervisor so that he would give me the route for that day. I made the routine inspection; check the level of oil, water, also the brake fluid, and finally the air pressure on the tires. While I was checking the tires, I noticed the edge of the tires had a lot of wear on them; they were so worn that you could see the wire on the inside of the tires.

I followed the safety protocol, and headed to the maintenance workshop, to report anomalies detected on the tires. The maintenance supervisor left his office and checked the tires. I asked him in writing for a change of tires; after the second inspection by him and his technicians, he denied my request and ordered his personnel to rotate the tires. They assured me that the tires were in perfect condition, which I could not contradict my supervisor, so, I proceeded to fill out my revision report, and they signed it. Without more than talking with the technicians, board the vehicle and left the terminal, I prepared to drive the 300 miles for my shift. For security reasons, the company changed routes daily and gave us a map to follow or we merely followed our supervisor. Usually, the route always led us to the mountains of San Bernardino. My shift started at 2:00 in the afternoon, and ended at 9:00 at night.

When I left the terminal, I turned on the radio, to listen to the traffic and weather report. Broadcasters announced a massive snowstorm in the San Bernardino Mountains. I notified my route supervisor, and he responded by saying that it was not true. Apparently, he did not care about our safety and forced us to climb the mountains. One of my colleagues preferred to return to the terminal and ask for another route to complete his shift. But when I enquired about doing the same thing, my boss threatened to fire me. I depended on my work, and I could not say no, with a little fear I went up the road. At the top of the mountain, you could see dark clouds, and there was thunder along with lightning. There was a moment when the sky was completely dark, and the rays of the sun pierced a few clouds. These changes in nature awoke my senses. I was taking in all the lightning, sounds of thunder, and the aroma of the pines.

For a moment my mind was lost in nothingness, thinking so many beautiful things of my youth. It seemed a strange presence was upon me; As if it were my last day of life, I do not know why I felt that way. What I can attest my mind was disconnected from reality, and my thoughts did not make sense. It felt like I was in a multi-dimensional reality as my mind relived events from my past. I felt that there would be a door to another dimension, where there is no death, and it felt as though these dimensions were simultaneously upon me, as more memories poured into my mind and my foot stepped on the accelerator, I wanted my car to detach from the pavement, and then I could take flight into those realms of the unknown.

Right then, I unconsciously slowed down the car, and extended my arm to turn off the radio, so I could listen to the noise of the water hitting the hood of the vehicle, also watched as the water run down the windshield. With the speed of the car, the drops separated and transformed into small particles of snow.

I tried to concentrate on the road since I didn't want to lose control of the car. I saw distant lightning that fell from the sky and hit an electric tower, followed by a deafening roar, which made the earth and myself rumble. As I continued driving through the storm, I realized I needed gas, so I stopped to fill the fuel tank, and also to wait for the other drivers. While getting gas, I went into the station to buy a coffee and a sandwich. When walking out of the building, my view focused on the movement of the trees, "Nature can be so beautiful!" I exclaimed. I sat down on a nearby bench and pulled a cigarette out of my pocket. That's when my supervisor arrived and told me that he only had fifteen minutes to get fuel. I put the cigarette to the ground and stepped on it with my foot. I became aware of all my senses, I heard the sound of the flames from the hot cherry on the cigarette sizzle when it went out, and I saw how the smoke expanded into the wind.

I waited for the other drivers and when they finally arrived at the gas station, I bought a coffee for each one of them. After the fifteen minutes of rest, we all returned to our route. Some people who were at the gas station advised us to wait until it stopped snowing. They believed that it was hazardous to drive under the current weather conditions since there was very little visibility on the road. Again the supervisor gave us the exit signal, this time I decided to drive more slowly. I remembered that my tires were not in good condition, the roads were slick so I did not exceed thirty miles per hour.

We continued descending off the mountain, and visibility was low, and also it was getting dark. Then suddenly I lost control of my car, I had no traction, and it was useless to try to stop it; it seems to pass over a layer of black ice. And the inertia and speed of the car pushed me off the road. I sensed that the vehicle hit the mountaintop, and began to shoot in the air. It was impossible to control and stop it; I was about to hit the ground from several feet high. It was going to be a certain death. I remember that I received a blow to my head and for a moment I lost all knowledge of my situation. By instinct, I clung to the wheel and did not let go.

There were so many bursts that the car gave on the pavement, that this caused all the glass of the windows to shatter. I only heard the noise of the glass, and the metal grinding when carving the asphalt. There was a moment when I felt that I was leaving the car, the only thing I did was pray and ask God for help. Suddenly the vehicle came down again on its four wheels, but it kept moving, sliding swiftly across the snow. I tried to brake but my effort was still useless, the brakes did not respond. Suddenly I felt a blow on my back, and the car stopped moving, I closed my eyes and fell unconscious for a few minutes. Miraculously I heard the voice of one of my coworkers, and he screamed fearfully, "Jesús, Jesús !"

He ran to the car and tried to help me, but he could not. I could not move my body I felt immobile as a sea of blood ran down my face, I also felt extreme pain in my back, it seemed that I had metal buried in my spine. I could not move my feet, and the blood kept running all over my body. I do not know how much time went by, but for me, it was an eternity. Suddenly the car went up in flames and my coworkers shouted without stopping, "Help us! Help!" Another driver saw the wreck and ran to help me get out of the car, he cut the seat belt with a knife, and took hold of both my arms and pulled me out of the car. In his desperation to get me away from the car before it exploded, he threw me to the side of the road, and shouted: "Do not fall asleep, do not fall asleep!"

My companions surrounded me, and they kept me conscious, and they got me into the car of the Good Samaritan who just rescued me from the burning vehicle. He had already called the paramedics. I was screaming in pain and asking for medical help. I could hear the sirens as the paramedics approached. After a brief evaluation of my injuries, they put me on a stretcher and transported me to a hospital. While in the ambulance, they gave me an injection to calm the pain. One of the paramedics was talking to me, telling me not to fall asleep. In an effort to keep me awake he asked me many questions; my date of birth, my name, where I lived, etc... He told me to move my feet, but I could not move them. I just felt a tingling sensation on my legs and heels. I felt that I might be paralyzed.

I heard the voices of the Paramedics very far away. I remember I told them that I felt a piece of metal jammed in my back. They said I didn't have anything in my back, that it was only a sensation that I felt. I lost the notion of time and when we got to the emergency room, the doctors quickly took me down to receive some x-rays, along with a full-length tomography (MRI). They did not find any fracture in my body; they only found six dislocated discs in my back. They explained to me that that was the reason why I felt a metal embedded in my back.

Miraculously, I arrived home the next morning, and rested for only a couple of hours; my supervisor summoned me to his office to talk about the accident.

I requested to speak with the general manager of the company. The GM of the company blamed me for the accident. I said goodbye and returned home and went in search of a lawyer. I found one in the yellow pages. I called him to make an appointment, the next day I went to see the lawyer, and he took my case.

I didn't even know what to think about life; there are so many challenges that destiny has. I thought life was not fair and blamed God. I took a moment to recapitulate my life, remembering the death of my daughter Brandy, the separation of my wife; and now I lost my job. My future was uncertain, and without direction, I felt miserable with the desire to die. I had nothing more to lose in this life, and nothing more to live for. I took refuge in prayer, and every day I asked God to help me. Finally, God sympathized with me, and He was the one who helped me get out of that terrible

68

depression. He made me a strong, healthy and wise person, He gave me the determination to overcome all the problems. As time passed, the physical and emotional wounds healed. I tried to see the positive through all my suffering. And did my best to take advantage of my situation.

While I was waiting for my lawyer to close my case, one day in the morning after my physical therapy; I went to speak to a community college counselor at Pasadena City College. I thought it was a good idea, to make the most of my time. After the counselor heard my situation, she evaluated my case and gave me a curriculum. The counselor asked me, "What do you like to study? And I responded, "Mathematics, I would like to be a Mathematician." She gave me a brochure and a plan to follow to achieve my academic goal.

My first semester at school was a bit difficult since I only thought about the terrible scenes of my accident. Sometimes I could not sleep all night, and because of sleeplessness, I couldn't get into my classes. And then, add that I was taking medication for depression, back pain and for sleeping; I was practically over medicated to the level of a zombie. I tried to make sure that this situation did not limit me and I made a great effort to pass all my subjects. The months passed and I continued to undergo medical treatment and physical therapies. My mediated condition did not improve, and the doctors suggested I have a surgery; to correct the dislocated discs in the spinal cord. They explained the risks to me, and they told me that I had a 50 percent chance of being left unresolved.

When I heard the risk of the surgery, I automatically said no. I could not take that risk, for me it was better to bear the headaches and backache. The risk of not being able to walk was very high. My thoughts overtook me, and I thought again that it was another punishment from God. I became strong-willed, and I made the decision not to let myself be defeated. To calm my mind I clung to my studies and kept a positive attitude. I stopped thinking about the misfortunes, and I learned to live every day as if it were the last day of my life. I could no longer sit in a chair to cry and complain to God, but on the contrary to heal, and spiritually to be able to overcome the trauma.

I spend the first year after my accident, doing my general education at school. Tried my best to get good grades, to earn a scholarship. Apart from studying at school, in my spare time, I read books on Theology, Metaphysics and other Philosophical subjects. I had a hunger to read as many books as possible, learn and to be able to discover the mysteries of the universe and our origin. That desperation to decipher the mysteries of life turned me into a book addict. During this time of my life, all my mental faculties were exceptionally receptive to all kinds of information, and my brain felt like a sponge as I absorbed more knowledge. For two consecutive years, I excelled in the subject of Molecular Biology, received recognition at the Pasadena College. My research project was an innovation at that time.

My ideas were unique and perceptive; which helped me get the best grades in the "Bio-Technology" program. And thanks to that effort I achieved my goal, to be the best student in the Latino community at my school. I was one of the few to receive honors in the Department of Natural Sciences. All those achievements were the result of my dedication and discipline. Well, I have to thank two great people, who were the pillars in my studies. Dr. Johnston and Dr. Kosmisky were the only people who truly believed in me and my talent. And that is why today I honor them by mentioning their names in this book.

I remember my first day in the MESA program, Dr. James Kosmisky interviewed me, and during the interview, he noticed that I had talent and dedication towards my future. After he interviewed me, he granted me a letter of reference and ordered me to bring it to the registry office. And that was all I needed to be an official member of his program. As the semesters passed, I was more passionate about my studies; specifically, in Mathematics, Physics, and Biology, these three branches of science interested me; since Natural Science was what intrigued me, it was easy for me to learn. This was another stage of my life, and the most important of all, since it is not easy in a foreign country, to be an outstanding student.

My persistence led me to be one of the best students in the MESA program; and thanks to that, I won the trust of Professor Dr. Kosmisky. As a prize for the effort of all the members of the program, the Professor took us to the Technological Institute of Technology (Caltech). We stayed three days in that prestigious University, for my good fortune, I had to sleep next to the room; where, many years ago, Albert Einstein had stayed. My life was transformed little by little, thanks to my achievements in my studies. This stage of my life gave me a moment of reflection, and I realized how close I was to reaching my goal. Nobody but God helped me change the course of life, with the help of God; I felt that there was nothing impossible to achieve. After having arrived in this country, and without speaking a word of English, I now saw the results of being a person of good moral conduct.

That was the best gift for myself that I could ever achieve, something to celebrate my triumphs.

I contemplated the gardens of Caltech and imagined what went through Albert Einstein's mind when he was also there. Now I started to enjoy my triumphs, and I had already reached a level I had never imagined. My mind kept thinking about Albert Einstein's room, I wondered what that great genius was thinking when he stayed in that simple room. I think that he was a humble person. Locked away in that room were many mysteries of the private life of Albert Einstein. Being in that place I understood, that my studies should be extraordinary, to be able to become like Albert Einstein, I knew that it was ironic to compare myself with such a genius. But only so I could understand my purpose in this life.

The second day of being at Caltech, Dr. Kosmisky and other teachers of the institute administered an I.Q and Personality examination. My result in I.Q.-Personality was one of the best, according to the results; I belong to three percent of the population of the United States. I did not understand very well, to which they referred to that result; the only thing I remember is the following; they separated me from the group, they took me to a private office. The Professors gave me more details about my results.

Maybe what I'm going to say is absurd, but the truth is; I never expected such favorable results. I was speechless for a moment; it was so much to my astonishment that I did not know what to say about it. But at the same time I cried with happiness, I longed for my family to be present to celebrate together. Of my whole family, only my brother (Francis) lived in Pasadena California, the rest of my family lived in Mexico and Texas. When I gave the news to my mother, you could imagine my disappointment when she told me, "I don't believe you! You're dreaming! Stop fantasizing." That wasn't what I wanted to hear from her. I expected a word of encouragement and support.

My mother did not stop insulting me, according to her I was not able to progress. One of her insults I still carry in my mind is my mother and my brother told me, "Stop lying and go to reality, it is not possible that you being a Mexican is capable of so much." Even my sister in law, the wife of my brother, she went to investigate with my school Professors. They wanted to be sure that I was not lying. The mental poverty, of some of my relatives, keeps them in the middle ages; which is hard to break, but I never would let myself be influenced by their negative comments.

On the contrary all that negativity, I transformed into positive energy. I continued with my studies practically alone, without the moral support of my family. Only my books, an Angel and God were my friends and my moral support.

Now that I mention my best friends, I can never forget about the professor Dr. Johnston, she was the director of Bio-Tech at Pasadena City College. He and his team were the pioneers in Cloning. His program was one of the most recognized in all of California. Thanks to his support, I achieved my goal of being the best student in your class. He saw my potential and gave me a letter of recommendation, to work in the Biology laboratories at Caltech, (California Institute of Technology). Before sending me to the lab, Dr. Johnston gave me several tips, and the letter, which at the bottom read, "Due to completing my program with the highest honors, now your future will be successful!" With that letter, my dream would come to pass; to work and study in that prestigious school. At that same moment, it came to my mind, that day when Dr. Kosmisky took me as a guest to Caltech. My work in the laboratory consisted of assisting three scientists in their research. At the same time that I was working, I learned new cloning techniques, executed by different scientists; and those new techniques I used in my research studies.

This new experience opened doors in the educational field for me. On some occasions I was invited to private institutions, to train teachers that did not understand the function and processes of cloning. Thanks to these new opportunities, my life changed, and I felt fulfilled by my efforts. For a moment I thought I lived it in excess; honestly, all this exceeded my expectations. These achievements and challenges brought with them new experiences. I will never forget one time I was invited to UCLA, Department of Biology by Dr. Johnston to train students and professors in the field of Cloning. When I received the invitation from my teacher, I graciously and humbly accepted it.

For one week, we were demonstrating new cloning techniques. Also, Professor Dr. Johnston presented one of my research presentations for training other professors. And upon seeing my work, one Professor rudely asked me, "Is this your work? Or did you copy it from another author?" That question was an insult, but I understood that they did not know my intellectual capacity, and I responded humbly, and I only said, "Intellect cannot be bought in hardware stores." I knew beforehand that intellectual racism existed everywhere in the world, but I never thought that I would experience it at this level in my lifetime. Some could not believe that I was privileged for my achievements. My studies were complex, and I always tried hard to be the best student in my school. I made sacrifices for my education, and I took it very seriously.

Those moments of frustration led me to get away from people and create my world for me to live in. Most of my free time was devoted to my studies. My daily routine began at 7 in the morning and ended at 11 or 12 at night, where I forced my mind to learn more. I did that for a little more than two years, the consequences of this were almost fatal. One of those many days of hard study I felt ill, maybe because I did not rest enough, or maybe because of my poor diet. Or perhaps a combination of both. But, I was addicted to reading and could not stop. I wanted to read more and more; to the point of almost having panic attacks, and I would suffer from anxiety; I needed to learn more and to understand more, so to control those moments of panic, I decided to lock myself in my room, without realizing the time I had spent more than a week locked up, and all I did was read.

One day during one of those episodes of isolation and locking myself in my room, I remember the phone ringing, when answering the call, I heard the voice of one of my teachers, her name was Mary Flowers. She gave me good news; that the Biology department had a job offer for me. Minutes later I left my apartment and went to school. When I arrived at Mrs. Flowers' office, she congratulated me and told me that I was the right candidate for that position. Then she handed me a job application and told me to bring it to the

Human Resources department, and she gave me the name of the person who would interview me. When I left her office, I was crying with happiness, because that was my dream. Since my first day of service as an assistant, I knew that I wanted to be employed by that prestigious school.

I walked to the cafeteria and sat down at a table to fill out the application. After contemplating the application, I headed towards the human resources office. While walking through the gardens of Caltech, my mind was distracted for a moment by listening to the singing of the birds. I decided to sit on a bench for a few minutes as I wanted to enjoy the cheerful song and rhythm of the birds as if it were a symphony. After a while I continued walking, when I passed the bookstore, I saw a man taking cans out of a trash can. It came to my mind that day when I entered this country, with nothing, not to forget the days I slept in the streets, and all the times I ate in community missions. At that moment I understood that my determination and my faith in God is the power of my existence. Finally, I thought the following; "Now, I won't ever have to worry about living in the streets, and being a nobody." It was time to enjoy life, and realize all my dreams have come true.

Upon arrival at the human resources office, I delivered my application to the receptionist. I told her that I was sent on behalf of Mary Flowers, she took my application and told me that they would call me in two or three days. I left the office headed home, and then I decided I wanted to celebrate and was looking for my friend Charlie. Luckily I found him in his apartment, I invited him to eat, and I told him what the reason for my happiness was. He accepted my invitation and we went to lunch at the Cheesecake Factory. We arrived at the restaurant and asked for a table overlooking the street. He congratulated me and told me never to stop being humble because achievements and triumphs are only temporary in life. We raised a glass of wine and made a toast to our friendship.

Upon conversation, I confided in him about my study habits. He advised me to take care of my health and to try to rest my mind so as not to get sick. I told him that I would try to sleep, but that it was impossible since my mind does not rest for a moment. When I finished eating I asked for the bill, then we got up from the table, left the restaurant and said goodbye. As soon as I arrived back at my house I continued studying, I had a philosophy book, and I started reading it. The hours passed and I could not stop reading, so I stayed just reading it for two or three more day's non-stop until I finished the book.

I received notice that I got the job and I arrived on Monday, and I went to work preparing a series of solutions for the group of scientists. I received a call from Human Resources; they had some questions for me. I went to the office, I reported to the receptionist immediately. Then in a few moments, the person who had assisted me commented that they had found an error in my application. Apparently, my Social Security Number did not match the name registered in the offices of the Government. Upon receiving this bad news, I found myself in need of speaking the truth and told him that I did not have a valid Social Security number, and did not have legal documents to work in this country.

She told me that they could help me, and made an appointment with the school attorney. A few days later I received a letter, indicating the time and date of my meeting with the lawyer. Again I felt happiness, thinking that they would possibly help me obtain my permanent residence. On the day of the appointment, I arrived with a positive attitude, when the lawyer interviewed me; he only asked me a few questions, relevant to my immigration status. One of the questions he asked was, "How did you enter this country?" I was honest in my response and told him how I crossed the border without documents. Which he did not like and laughed at me, he grimaced, left his chair and told me to wait a moment.

After fifteen minutes, he returned and he said he was very sorry, that my situation was very complicated and that at the moment they could not help me. When I entered the country without a visa, I became a criminal in the country. He explained how the immigration laws worked in the U.S.A. In conclusion, I was not eligible to receive a work permit. Then he continued saying. "You know that I can call the immigration authorities, and they can deport you back to your country of origin." Finally, he told me that this was my last day at school and in the laboratory.

It was impossible for me to believe, that in a few minutes my life took a 360-degree turn. And in that second my sandcastle collapsed. Throwing me to the floor and among its rubble, all my efforts, of almost three years of studies; I did not know what to think at that moment. I just thought it was not fair, and sometimes the plans do not go as planned. Devastated and bewildered, I said goodbye to the lawyer. I thanked him for his services and I headed towards the exit door.

At Pasadena California Institute of Technology; Artificial DNA Pool

Before leaving, he told me; "Jesús, you know that you can come back to our institution, and work with us, the day you get your work permit." I just smiled and thanked him again, left his office as soon as I could. I felt lost for a moment, and I could not find words of encouragement, to console myself.

As I walked back, my mind became distracted when I saw the school gardens, I sat next to an artificial fountain, and I asked God for wisdom to overcome this challenge.

At that moment of reflection, I realized that God's trials are tough to accept. Only strong, intelligent people can overcome them. That was the only thing that came to my mind, although it was not what I wanted to live or feel, after a moment I returned to my reality. There was nothing else to do; I just had to resign myself to the situation. A couple of hours passed and I decided to go back home, I felt angry inside. I walked to the main street and boarded the bus back home. When I climbed up, I sat in the back and started talking loudly. The bus driver told me to keep quiet because people had complained about my behavior. "Fine!" I said in a loud voice, "Let me off the bus I will walk home!"

The road became eternal, but after an hour I finally got home. I walked to the refrigerator and got some water, and then I put a tape in the VCR, the title of the video was "Galielo's - Battle for the Heavens" A Documentary. Every time I felt depressed, I tried to distract my mind and watching these exciting kinds of videos entertained my mind. I felt like the same character, "Galileo" when in during his best times as a scientist and philosopher, is when he was condemned the most. Because it's simple to be smarter than those doing the condemning.

I spent the rest of the day watching several videos of that same guy, and my mind kept thinking, how difficult life is; for undocumented people in this country. Only a couple of weeks were left until the semester ended at school. Even if I completed and obtained a university degree, I could not work in any school in the

United States. After meditating on everything that happened, I decided not to go to school anymore. I felt defeated. Considering my situation, I thought it was the best option at that moment.

The only thing left for me to do was thank Dr. Johnston. Since he was the one that recommended me in the Caltech Laboratory. Three days later, I went to look for him at his office, and I told him my situation. He was surprised by what happened, and he told me that he was very sorry. When I said goodbye to him, I decided to stop by the school library. I wanted to feel that adrenaline, and the feeling of being accepted at school one last time. I sat at a table and watched the students roaming from one place to another searching for books, desperate to finish their tasks, or waiting for a computer station to open up.

I noticed one student who was scratching his head with a look of frustration, and I asked him if I could assist him? He said, "I cannot solve this math problem." I took a moment to explore the concept of the problem and then I explained to him how to solve it.

We started in a conversation where he confided in me that he also did not have a valid Social Security Number. He had paid for his books and classes in cash because he could not get a student loan because his parents came to America when he was a small boy. I gave him the name of Dr. Kosmisky, and I also told him the department where he could find him, I told him maybe he could help. Finally, I said goodbye to him and went to check out some books to take home. When I took the books in my hands, the tears came out, I could not believe that it would be the last time that I would use my student library card to check out books. The library was for me a refuge, during all those years of hard study. I will never forget that magical place.

I stood there and contemplated what I was feeling. I understood many things about life, at a young age. I took some books on Philosophy and Religion, and I promised myself to never to read of Natural Sciences again.

My thoughts turned to fantasy as I wondered what it would be like if I had my papers. And those kinds of ideas created questions like, "What about if I had finished my degree in Molecular Biology? Maybe I could have discovered a cure or treatment for people who are ill from a disease."

This situation was taking a heavy toll on me, I wasn't going to let it defeat me so easily, and I knew I had to act wisely and be strong since this was not the first time something terrible had happened to me. I take refuge in knowing that there is a unique and True God, who has always been by my side to help me over the bumps of life. So I decided to start with a new plan to read books on Philosophy and locked myself in my apartment for seven consecutive days. I read the books of the Authors, Immanuel Kant and David Hume. These two great philosophers are my favorites, after reading their books, my mind expanded on the concepts of, metaphysics, theology and also of the ideas postulated on the theory of knowledge. And through this I came to understand that our existence and position in the universe is somewhat paradoxical since our mind cannot differentiate between reality and fiction; consequently, our dreams are a mark of eternity, and that reality is fiction. After those seven days of confinement and reading, I understood that naivety was to blame for my problems. Feeling confident in my decisions, I decided to go back to school, to deliver the keys to the laboratory where I once worked. When leaving my house, everything seemed normal around me. I arrived at the school and gave the call to my supervisor Mary Flowers. She told me that she was very sorry about everything and that she would like to help me and to know about my future plans.

I did not answer anything to her because I was still uncertain about my future. I left the laboratory to eat in the school cafeteria, after lunch I returned to my house; when I arrived at my home I felt dizzy, and my vision became blurry. I could not concentrate on what I was doing, and my body trembled, in my desperation, I tried to call my brother, but his phone line was busy. Without thinking about what I was doing, I took a few coins in my hands and went running to the street in search of a public phone booth. I arrived at the Public Library, went up the stairs to the entrance and headed towards the telephones. I tried to insert the coins in the phone, but for some reason, my eyesight was so blurred I could not get the coins in. My head was spinning and after several attempts to insert the coins on the pay phone, I was failing. I decided it was better to walk to my brother's house.

I went back down the stairs to the street, and when I got to the last step, my eyes did not recognize the objects around me, everything became multicolored, it seemed that I was inside a rainbow and couldn't get out. My mind was confused, I had never experienced something like this. Only in dreams, I had had those perceptions or vices, but now they were real. From one moment to another my mind entered into a new dimension. My body felt very limp, and I felt as my spirit was separating from my body. In those moments of uncertainty, I looked at two places at once, one was the physical world and the second was the metaphysical world.

With this explanation, I do not mean that one can exist, in two places at the same time because the body and the spirit are a single entity. I could no longer interact or respond to the physical world, I heard a very strong squelch, and I realized that the sound came from the sky. I raised my eyes and saw a very bright light, which came out from a cloud, and from that cloud, I saw my Angel Miguel. I recognized him, my Angel, and I called him by his name, he smiled and came toward me. He was my protective Angel, that same Angel who had manifested on the border when I first came to America. He also recognized me and mentioned my name, took my hand and lifted my spirit from the ground, he said, "Follow me, let's go see my father, God."

When my spirit left my body, I felt an intense heat inside my being. I also felt that my heart was beating very slowly, and little by little it stopped beating. My mind relaxed, and I was relieved to see the Angel next to me. All the chaos of my body and the city suddenly transformed into peace and harmony, and I didn't seem to care what happened around me, now the only thing I wanted was to embrace that Angel, who strongly pronounced my name and calmed me down. I let him guide me between that rainbow, and we were very close to the heaven, but my spirit had already abandoned my body. And the Angel directed me towards the tunnel of light, at the entrance of the tunnel, I observed four Cherubim with wings; and at the bottom of the light tunnel was a golden throne, it was very far off in the distance, but I could see that it was being carried, with The Father sitting on the throne.

The Angel told me to "put myself down on the floor" I threw myself down, and I saw my body; indeed it lay there lying in the street where I left it, and two Angeles guarded it, they were attentive to what happened around me. I asked the Angel next to me, "Do I have two spirits?" He answered; "One of them belongs to the heart, which is judged by God according to your works, and the second belongs to the spirit of God, which is eternal and brings you to the resurrection." We continued through the entrance to the tunnel; I was anxious to see the great city of God.

Being in front of the tunnel, I perceived an aroma of fresh roses, which came from the Angel and Cherubim. I also saw the ritual of doing the Cherubim, to light the incense burners that are in the main entrance of the city of God. I heard a powerful voice, the voice said, "My son, come to me, I want to touch your head. And the Angel let go of my hand and told me to walk alone, to the presence of God. I felt a force of pure energy emanate, that penetrated my being as if that light of life took over my spirit and connected with my mind. I felt a warm hand on my head, and God said; "Go back to your house, I will be observing your works on earth. It is not yet time for you to enter my kingdom, return to the physical world and await my next sign."

When I started to return to the physical world, the Angel guided me back, I took two hands and pray for my soul. After praying the Angel said, "Follow me and I will take you to your body, and on the way, I will tell you things about your existence in the metaphysical world, I will give you an explanation, that maybe in this moment you do not understand it; but in the future, you will understand everything perfectly. The metaphysical world is a real dimension, persuaded only by your eternal spirit, in which God himself lives. And only in the presence of us can the Angels perceive. At the end of getting out of the sky and out of the tunnel of light, my body recovered the knowledge and I got up with the help of the two Angels. I turned my eyes for the last time to heaven and I saw my Angel wave goodbye to me. He was moving away little by little waving his hands. And in an instant, the cloud of light dissipated into the Sun. It took me a while to recover my senses, I could not distinguish any object. All the objects that my mind perceived were in a constant movement; everything seemed to be echoes of its components that were fabulous colors mixed like a rainbow. Spiritually this is the metaphysical state of all things, as vibrant energy.

That metaphysical state is the reality of God and the pure knowledge of pre-established harmony. There is no other logical explanation to that phenomenon, that is the fifth dimension; where everything is mixed with the Divine Quantum Energy, and its conductor of that Universal Energy is Gravity. That Gravity is the one that contains in its hands, the mystery and the principle of all things in the universe. Even time and space are nothing without this Divine ingredient. After this though, I returned to my reality, thanks to the Angeles that sprinkled water on my face; and I began to recover.

After I woke up, I saw how the Angels became people. They took me in their hands and dragged me off the ground and sat me on the sidewalk. And then they took me to my house when we got to my apartment, they came in with me, one of them asked me, "Why do you have so many books? I told him that I liked to read. Another of the Angels took my writings and reviewed them, as he was reviewing them, he told me, "Your writings are fascinating, take a pen and paper, because I will dictate some of the secrets of the kingdom of God." I did as I was told and the Angel began to dictate to me, themes about the spirit of God and his supernatural strength that runs throughout the universe.

I took note of everything I needed to know. The Angels were in my apartment for seven consecutive days, so I had the opportunity to ask more than a thousand questions related to humanity. They advised me to remember, all the symbols that God had shown me in my first encounter with Him. Those symbols contain all the secrets; now it is in you that you understand their meaning. But before your last encounter with God, you will find the right meaning of all the symbols, and God will be filled with happiness when you meet with Him.

As the seven days passed, the Angels filled me with wisdom, in this seven days I confirmed to comprehend the existence of the Angels. They helped me to reason their presence on the physical and metaphysical level, and they explained it to me in this way; "When you close your eyes you can detach yourself from your physical reality and enter that other metaphysical reality, and in that metaphysical world, you can interact with the living and the dead. That means that the real world of intelligent beings, is composed of a harmony pre-established by God, in the quantum metaphysical world and its eternal energy emanates in a wave of gravity, expanding throughout the universe, controlling the will of the humans and all living beings."

Here is where the actual knowledge of the theory of knowledge, and the truth about all things are real. This new concept of perceiving things is intra-rational, "an interior", which corresponds to the emanation of knowledge of God. Suddenly with this thought in my mind, I was interrupted for a moment, the Angels asked me to stop writing, and ordered me to go out with them to walk to a park. I left with them from my apartment, and as we walked through the streets and alleys, the Angels showed me the outside world from another perspective, and they asked me many questions. They said it was vital for me to differentiate between the physical world and the metaphysical world. That morning our walk started in front of Fuller College of Theology, and it finished at the Church of Saint Andrew. After walking, we returned to my house, again I was ordered to write everything I had lived and perceived. I was able to return to my normality, my mind was stable again. I no longer had any fear, no anxiety; I just wanted to be writing the Divine things that the Angeles shared with me. Try to make some comparisons, with what I already knew about the physical world and metaphysical, but my mind did not understand at all.

After seven days, the Angels left and I continued to write and remember what I had lived with them. When I finished writing what happened, I decided to visit my Doctor. I made an appointment and went to see him, and I told him everything that I had lived, and he told me that many times this happens to people, who do not eat well and they study too much. The stress to strain the brain and bring it to its limits is not good, because it can be counterproductive. What you saw, could happen to anyone, so take care of your health. Finally, the Doctor told me, "Try not to study as much or else you can end up in the hospital, because of an anxiety attack."

I followed the instructions of my Doctor, and it seems that this method of living without so much stress helped me to feel better because since then I have not fallen again. But, if I was clear about what I experienced; that living experience was my second encounter with God, occasioned by forcing my mind in search of Divine knowledge. After I had survived, I knew that God had something else for me, and I took it as a second chance to live. Even though this episode almost took my life, I had to overcome it in some way, and I took advantage of it as a pretext, to thank God for that joy of having allowed me to witness His majesty and those of his Angels and Cherubim.

For a whole week, I had dreams in which the three Angels revealed to me more secrets of life. And they told me that other trials and challenges would come harder, but that I would be prepared for everything. There will also come a third encounter with God; and that encounter will be the last in your physical life. We cannot reveal to you when that last experience will be, what we do know is the following; "Before that meeting, you will live seven years preparing yourself spiritually, and after that preparation, you will be able to reach the precession of God.

After that, your spirit will become pure light. And you will live eternally in heaven. You will be like the Morning Star. "This Angel's message left me more anxious to learn, and at the same time, I asked myself, "How will it be my last encounter with God? Where will it be? I dared to ask more questions to the Angels, look them in the eyes and remained mute. Seeing my reaction with the Angels, they preferred to say goodbye to me. Now I would have to continue to live a normal life, and I will try to understand all these events and dreams.

I decided to travel to Las Vegas Nevada since my son Jesse lived there. I talked to my son Jesse's mom, and I told her I was preparing my things to move to Vegas. She got excited and gave me words of encouragement since she wanted me to be close to our son. She also told me that Las Vegas was a new growing city and that there were many job opportunities. I said I would arrive in a couple of days. I packed my belongings, rented a truck, and I said goodbye to my friends. I told them that I had a mission to fulfill in Vegas, but that I did not know how things would happen. They just laughed at me, and they said good luck. At last, I thought, that God gives everyone a mission, and it is in us to carry out that mission, otherwise, we will never grow spiritually. And if we want to enter the kingdom of God, we have to do his will.

On my way to Vegas, I stopped several times to rest and refuel. And at the same time to contemplate the stars, I have always been fascinated to see the stars at night. I thought about when I was a child and went out to the patio of my house to look at the stars at night. My trip to Las Vegas lasted seven hours, which served as a time of reflection on my life.

Chapter Six

My emotional and spiritual life

All human beings of all the universe are in search of happiness, and some of us have had to travel thousands of miles to find it. To me in particular, destiny brought me to the city of Las Vegas, Nevada; to find happiness next to my now new found wife, Sue Prinzen. When I arrived in Las Vegas, I found a small oasis in the desert; the city measured about 12 miles north by 12 miles east, almost 144 square miles. In comparison with Los Angeles or the City of Mexico, it is relatively small. It was July in the Year 2005 when I relocated in this city, I rented an apartment, and I also got a job. I also enrolled in the University, (UNLV) to start a career in Business Administration.

When I visited the UNLV campus, I was informed of the prices of the classes, and of the cost of the materials and then compared them to the cost of going to CSN (College of Southern Nevada) then compare the prices of both schools. I discovered that the CSN classes were cheaper, and not to get out of my budget, I enrolled in school, even though I had already been accepted at UNLV. After transferring my credits, and talking to a school counselor, I was advised to continue my career in Science; since I only needed a few credits to obtain a Master's degree. But I said that I was no longer interested in studying science. The counselor did not like my answer, but I was not going to sit down with him to explain the reason for my decision.

My need and desire for improvement were so great that I chose to enroll in three different Colleges of Las Vega, CSN was one of them, in this college I studied Real Estate Law. The second college was called Kaplan; in that school I prepared myself, to obtain the license of Real Estate Agent (Realtor). Finally, I studied at Key Realty College, and I attended an apartment administration course. (Property management). My plans were, to become the best Broker in Vegas, and also to have a property management company. I thought that way I would earn enough money to live decently. I do not have another reason to study hard, thanks to my efforts. I passed the Real Estate exam in less than a month. After I got my Real Estate License, and my instructor referred me to the Coldwell Banker broker.

After meeting with the broker and a few hours later, I decided that they had what I was looking for to make my dreams come true in Real Estate. They trained me for five long months, and I became a Realtor. During this time I continued with my studies in the CSN School. In my place of work, I worked with Sue Prinzen. We made a good friendship, one day we went out for coffee. After a few months, that friendship transformed into romance, and after a year we married through the civil registry. Our wedding was simple, only a few of my wife's friends accompanied us to the celebration. That day my wife and I swore to eternal love.

We believed that God had united us, for a useful purpose in this life. It was as if a supernatural force joined us, without letting us separate. Just like metal attracted by a magnet, Sue and I shared many things in common. She liked to read Metaphysics books. And Philosophy books. For us, there was not a day that passed without reading a good book. She sat on the sofa overlooking the window facing the street, with a cup of tea in her hands, and me with a cup of coffee. Sometimes we rant about philosophical issues, but without getting angry, after all, we knew, that our opinion was only our speculation about it. One of the views of my wife was that "Our existence in the physical world is temporary, and it is only a process of spiritual evolution. For at the moment of death, our spirit joins the cosmic energy of God." (Sue Prinzen R.I.P 7.12.15)

I enjoyed our deep conversations, and I liked listening to her express herself in life. She was an awakened soul and had risen to very high spiritual levels. Another of her opinions, regarding the spiritual realms, was that; "Our existence in this physical world, is only a process of evolution, and the energy of our spirit, is like a radiant multicolored rainbow which is the origin of all things in the universe. Where the here and now come together, and are the cause of our existence." That was the philosophy of my beautiful wife Sue. I felt that God, after so many challenges, had compensated me by sending me a wife like Sue. She helped me forget all those moments of bitterness, also helped me see life from another perspective. So our amazing life together began as emotional and sentimental.

We both achieved great triumphs, which we celebrated to the fullest. I was living a new stage in my life, and I believed that those were the blessings of God, and to thank God for my wife. We used to go to the mountains and pray. But before going on a trip to the mountains, we always visited some elderly families who lacked food. My wife and I took the task of preparing food, and we took to the food to their apartments. After feeding them, we left on a journey, with a lot of humility. I mention this just one of charity towards the poor since we did it with all our heart without any interest in the middle. This was our way to thank God for our Blessings.

During the years that I lived with my wife, I understood that to be happy in this life, human beings, must live as a couple according to the traditions, and thus be part of a spiritual duality. Our being needs love, tranquility, and emotional stability. Keeping this in mind, it will help us to understand the right plans of God in our lives. I also realized and recognized that the triumphs do not come by themselves; it was the cause and effect produced by our actions. Our life experiences transform us, and our moods. How we relate to others. I never thought that within us humans, there was a sentimental side, covered by debris of pessimism.

This I say because; for me in previous years, I only wanted to study Science, to satisfy my ego. Now the moment of exploration had arrived, my true nature and true person. The first two years of my marriage were full of achievements and learning. Everything was going very well God had blessed us with a good job, and with a place to live. My wife and I always worked together, I was The Realtor, and she was The Loan Officer. A great Husband-wife team.

Until the day of August 20, 2008, my wife called me on the phone, to let me know where she was. She told me that she wasn't feeling well and fainted and that she had fallen off some stairs. I left my apartment quickly and went to find her. She had been working on the neighboring property, and when I arrived to help her, I saw her standing up, supported by a handrail. I was concerned and asked, "What's wrong with you? How do you feel?" She only asked me for water to drink. I gave her a bottle of water, but when trying to take the water, she could not hold the bottle in her hands. Her hands trembled uncontrollably, and her mouth could not get the water. I saw her in such a bad state that I suggested going to the Hospital, but she refused to go. She said she was just dizzy, and it would be fine. She decided to try and continue with her work, and a few hours later, she arrived home and went to bed, she asked me for two pain pills.

I ran to the bathroom to fetch the pills, along with some water; she took the pills and after a while she fell asleep. When I saw her resting and in a deep sleep, I went to sleep too. I laid at her side and hugged her, I fell asleep and around 11:00 pm. I heard a moan. I leaned in to her quickly and noticed that my wife could not breathe. I lifted her in my arms to help her breathe, but she could not, she just kept on moaning, with her right hand she gestured to me, and pointed to her throat, she told me that something was stuck in her throat. I desperately took the phone in my hands, and called the Paramedics.

I reclined on the bed again and quickly searched for her identification and insurance card in her handbag. The operator asked me for my wife's personal information. I tried to keep calm but seeing my wife in that condition so desperate I could not be calm. I gave all the details to the operator, and she told me that the Ambulance would arrive in seven minutes. In those moments of panic, and desperation, you feel that time doesn't move on. For me, those seven minutes were eternal, since I did not know what to do to help my wife. The only thing I could do was to keep my wife awake.

I propped her up to sit on the edge of the bed and when I heard that the paramedics arrived, I ran out to open the door, seeing the group coming in armed with medical machines I felt relief. I guided them to where my wife was. They quickly gave first aid. One of the paramedics asked me for my wife's full information. He also ordered me to draft the events that occurred. I took a pen and a paper and wrote what happened; I even told them that I had administered two Aspirins.

After the Paramedics examined my wife, they determined that it was just dizziness and they told me that it was nothing serious; but I was not very convinced of her diagnosis, and I asked them to please take her to a hospital for further testing. "It's nothing serious," said one Paramedic. I screamed "Don't bother! I'll take her in my car." Seeing my attitude, the paramedics decided to put her on a stretcher and transfer her to "Sunrise Hospital." Upon arrival at the Hospital, the ambulance entered the emergency area. When my wife saw the hospital building, she told me that it was not necessary to enter. I tried to calm her down, and I promised her that everything would be alright.

Once inside the hospital, they put my wife in a room. Five minutes later, several doctors came to her room to examine her. One of them was a Neurologist specialist. He ordered a CT scan and X-rays in the lungs. Everything was fine, the doctors said, suddenly the Neurologist returned and told me that my wife had to be intervened immediately. The nurses told me to leave the room; they had orders to prepare my wife for a terrible surgery.

Before leaving the room, I noticed that my wife began to tremble uncontrollably. The doctors took her quickly to the intensive care room. She lost consciousness. One of the nurses gave me the room number, to which she would be transferred, C214 ICU. I went to the waiting room of (ICU) "Intensive Care Unit." I waited almost 40 minutes to find out about my wife. The nurses only told me that it was very serious.

The same Nurse suggested that I go home to rest, but I could not leave my wife in that state. I stayed there in the waiting room until dawn, as they did not inform me of anything so far. I decided to ask in the nurses. Finally, a nurse explained my wife's condition, so that when I saw her, I would not be alarmed. "She is in a coma" I felt my soul split into a thousand pieces, I could not keep what I heard, and I refused to accept it. For a moment I thought it was a joke, but the Doctors confirmed what the nurse had said.

The same Doctor gave me details of the procedure they did to try and save her life. "Your wife was subjected to a small surgery, the purpose of the surgery is to drain blood that spilled into the brain which in turn gave her a massive stroke. One of her arteries inside her brain is not draining causing her to be in an induced coma." I got very nervous, and I was speechless for a moment, I did not know what to say or ask. I closed my eyes, and I asked God to help me in these difficult times. I continued in the waiting room praying for my wife's health, and an hour later informed me that I could stop by to see her.

The moment I entered her room, I saw her with many cables connected to her body, and a mechanical ventilator inserted into her windpipe. It was something surreal, I could not believe what I was seeing, I thought it was just a dream. Carefully, I crouched near her bed, as I knelt by her side I took her hand and spoke in silence. I asked God for wisdom to understand this situation. Then I got off the floor and hugged her, but she did not answer. I kissed her on her forehead and I could not contain my crying. Suddenly one of the Nurses on duty came in, and said, "Your wife may not survive, the CT scan analysis shows a lot of blood inside her skull. It was better to disconnect her from the machines so she would not suffer more." I felt a chill all over my body. This news was very disabling for me.

I did not know what to answer, and my mind was in shock for a moment, then the beautiful moments I lived with my wife flashed before my eyes. The first thing I remembered was the day of our wedding; June 30, 2006. All the details of that day were dancing in my mind.

That day she looked so beautiful entering the Church at the hand of her brother, walking down the aisle, and I stood in front of the altar, and I heard the sound of her heels, hitting the floor as she walked towards me holding a bouquet of flowers in her hands and I remembered her gown dragging on the floor behind her. When she stood next to me, I could not see her face clearly, because she had a white veil covering her face. Her brother lifted the veil when he got her to my side, and she smiled, looked me in the eye and told me she loved me. I answered by saying; "My love for you is immense, and you know that what I say is true." We both think in the same way, and we said together, "God is about to unite us forever." The minister was there before us, and we tied the knot, to unite in marriage. I felt a little nervous, but sure of what I was doing. When the celebration began, we came together to receive the blessing of God. They asked us about the rings, and before placing them on our fingers, the minister asked the last question, "Are you sure you want to take this step?" I answered, "Yes" and Sue also said yes. It was time to unite forever. I put her ring on her finger, and she put my ring on my finger.

We said our marriage vows and made a promise before God that we would love, honor and cherish each other until death do us part.

Suddenly, I was back at the moment. Seeing her laying there fighting for her life that was quickly coming to an end, I wanted to express to her my love, to tell her how I cherished her. And I promised her again that I would be with her until the last moment of her life; just as I promised on our wedding day.

After what seemed to be a long time, of reflecting and assimilating what the nurse said; but after the nurse saw I was slow to respond she asked, "Are you okay sir?" I heard the nurse say to me. I realized I had not replied to her as I was lost in a sea of emotions and my memories. I answered yes. But inside I was dying with my wife. According to the results, the CT scan revealed a high blood content, spilled inside her skull and that was the cause of the coma. God is the one with the last word, and if he decides to take my wife; I could not do anything about it. I felt that my faith in God was greater than ever.

That night I did not sleep for a minute, I was at the foot of my wife's bed. I did not want to leave her room, even though the Doctors and Nurses told me that I needed to rest. I could not stop observing my wife; I would talk to her frequently, but there was no reaction. By early morning I began to feel the fatigue in my body and returned home to try to sleep. Without realizing the time was already 7 in the morning. I had to work that day, and I called my boss to tell him what happened to my wife. He told me to take the whole day off.

Seven days passed and Sue did not wake up. Her situation became more critical minute by minute. The Doctors had to do something about it, that same day, the team of Doctors informed me, that they would have to remove part of the skull, to relieve the pressure off her brain. They told me there was no hope that she would recover. Even being transported to the operating room would be dangerous due to the movement and the exchange of oxygen tanks.

After listening to them, I asked them for a moment to make a decision. I left the room and went to the waiting room, I was in shock. I could not believe what was happening, One day we were happy and the next day she was in a coma, it was all too much for me to try and comprehend. I couldn't do anything, and the tears poured out of me like a waterfall. I became aware of several groups of people, and one of those groups caught my attention; because they were a group of seven people all dressed in white. About the time I took notice of them, one of the people dressed in white approached me and asked, "Is everything okay with your family?" I answered; "My wife's life is in danger." And they all surrounded me and prayed for me and my wife's health. Then the leader of the group said, "Do not fear Son of Man, we are Angels sent by God, and we are here to relieve your pain."

They laid their hands on my body, and I felt an inner peace like never before. Then they spoke in tongues, or a language unknown to me, but the spirit of God manifested! And I was filled with the same Spirit, and I was made me understand everything they said. They would not stop praying, and I would travel as their bodies emanated a light, forming an aura of energy that covered me. And I started to feel a warmth deep in my body. My mind concentrated on what they said. One of them spoke out loud, "We believe in the power of prayer, and we know that God has heard your request." And they continued to pray; "God almighty father, creator of all visible and invisible; Listen to our prayer, Lord." And it enabled my mind to understand what was happening with my wife. The prayers continued, "we are your servants oh Lord, hear our cries." At this time I was so moved by the prayers I cried out, "I ask you to heal my wife Sue, Amen."

When they finished praying, I felt an intense heat inside my being. My bones burned, my face and hands were wet from sweat.

The people who were praying for me told me that they felt the presence of God. And they ordered me to go talk to my wife, "Go tell her body to be healed, and speak with authority, demand her suffering cease" I obeyed them and immediately ran to my wife's room.

With all my might I walked in with a new found power, and with a voice of authority, I told my wife to "Be healed in the name of Jesus Christ." Before finishing the prayer, she tried to move her hand and to open her eyes. I told her not to strain that God had already heard my prayers.

I told her that she would come out well with the Surgery and that God had a purpose for her in my life. I was speaking in tongues, for a moment the Spirit of God manifested in my being. It was a very emotional moment, and when I finished praying, I called the Nurses and informed them that my wife was ready for the surgery. Now everything was in God's almighty hands, He and his Angels would be present next to the Doctors, guiding them at all times so that my wife would get well from her surgery. Those were all that I heard the Spirit of God put in my heart. And I could feel God was still present.

Before they wheeled her bed to the surgery room; I took her in my arms and I kissed her on the cheek. I left the room to walk between the corridors, I tried to calm down, but when I heard wounded people, complaining, I did not have peace of mind. Unconsciously I walked to the parking lot of the Hospital. I looked up at the sky and asked God, - Why do you send me more proof, Father? I am your faithful son, and I do not need more pain to understand the concept of life. But God had already responded to me by sending his Angels. Now I was just waiting. I started thinking about how ironic life is, my wife was perfectly fine a few days ago, and now she was caught between life and death.

I didn't see anything right in this, but I only asked God to heal her to share more years of life with her. At that moment I realized that the concept of life was deeper than I imagined. This experience made me understand the importance of love. I returned to the hospital. Finally, the doctors and their medical team said it was time for surgery; I accompanied them through the corridors. I remember how the medical team organized, to move my wife to the surgery room. That image is so painful for me, that I would like to erase it from my mind, but I have understood that God exposes us to events of trauma and happiness; so that we learn to value and evaluate life. What a painful way to understand life, seeing a loved one on the verge of death. And the most challenging thing is not being able to do anything about it.

I asked the Doctors and Nurses, to do everything possible to save my wife. The doctors told me to come back in four hours. I did not want to retire much from this place; I preferred to wait in the waiting room. One hour later I went to eat in the cafeteria. I bought soup and bread with coffee; I ate as fast as possible to return to the waiting room. I did not know what to do in that moment of anguish and despair. I wanted to be aware of what was happening with my wife in the surgery room. I had in my hands on a Bible and a Rosary, these two instruments for me possessed all the Divine power of God. To distract my mind I read the book of Luke, suddenly I saw between the corridors the group of people who had prayed with me in ICU.

Quickly I leaped out of the chair and went out into the hall to talk to them. And tell them that my wife was already in the surgery room. But when going out into the hall I did not see anyone, I thought that my mind was tired and that I saw visions. I walked between the corridors looking for them, and I did not find them. I saw a person coming out of the bathroom and asked him if he had seen a group of people go through there? He told me; "I have not seen anyone go through here." I returned to the waiting room and sat in the same chair. A few minutes later, a nurse came out and mentioned my name, told me, "Your wife, Sue, is out of danger, the

98

surgery was a success" I thanked God. The nurse hugged me, then told me to return to ICU to see my wife. I wanted to see my wife at that moment, and I went jogging down the corridor as fast as I could.

Suddenly the doors of the operating room were opened, and I saw a stretcher that was slowly protruding. It was my wife, and I shouted her name, "Sue!" And she turned to see me and smiled at me. The surgeon gave me the "thumbs up" sign, and nodded. At that moment I was filled with immense happiness, and I could not control my emotion, and I ran to the stretcher to touch my wife and reach out to take her hand.

But the Doctors puhed me away. They said; "You have to wait to see her." I kept walking along the side of the stretcher, until we reached the elevators, and I could not enter with her because they closed the door very fast. I pressed the button to take an elevator and get to my wife's room. I waited for two minutes or more, while those two minutes passed, the group I encountered earlier dressed in white came to mind. Maybe they were leaving the surgery room. As God had said through his Angels. "The Angels and I will be there guarding your wife."

What wonderful thoughts, now I was rising spiritually. I had never felt such a beautiful sensation inside my being. With every difficult or painful experience, I am taken to a higher Spiritual place. All I needed was for my wife to improve so that we could return home. I could not stop crying with joy. When I reached the room where my wife was, they instructed me to wait another thirty minutes while she recovered and they had her under observation. With my Bible and my Rosary in my hands, I paced through the corridors once again. Since my attitude had changed, I began to take things with great tranquility. And leave everything in the hands of God, because He is the one who has control of our lives, and He alone has the answers to all things because he created us before we were born. All my grief was gone when I saw my wife alive and with a smile on her face.

Finally, the thirty minutes passed and I went to room C214. Upon entering the room, my wife was awake waiting for me, and she signaled to me that she wanted to write. I took paper and a pen from my backpack and put a notebook under the paper and put her hand so she could write down what she wanted to tell me. The first thing she wrote was; "What happened to me and why am I here?" I told her that it was not the time to talk about that and stroked her hair. I told her to rest so that she could recover soon. She closed her eyes and fell asleep. I watched her and caressed her face. While she was sleeping, I left the room and went to the medical station to talk to the nurses. I asked them what their prognosis was. They told me that everything depended on a quick recovery and that very soon we would leave the Hospital.

Three months passed and my wife was still in the Hospital, her recovery was very slow. For me it was an eternity, my life changed forever. But I was content to know that my wife was out of danger and that God had not abandoned us at any time. My joy was enormous since my wife was a living miracle as was described by the specialists since the percentage of people who survive a massive cerebral stroke is very minimal.

Finally, my wife finished with all her therapies and was able to return home in November 2008. I already had the apartment prepared for her arrival. I remember when they brought her home, I did not have the wheelchair. When the ambulance arrived with my wife, I asked the paramedics to help me take her to the bedroom. But they said they could not, because they were in a hurry so they just left her on a chair in the living room. Half of her body was paralyzed, the left side to be exact. When the Doctors told me that my wife was ready to go home, I felt like the happiest person in the world, it seemed that God gave us another opportunity to be together. In this second stage of our marriage, I understood many things of life. God was conditioning me for all the changes in my life. Now I would have to take care of my wife - as she depended on me 100 percent. With half of her body paralyzed she was unable to do even simple tasks.

Love was all I could give, and I just asked God never to abandon me. Because without His strength I could not have done all the things I did for my wife. Taking care of my wife was more than a simple task since I had to work for a living. I was forced to talk to my boss and asked him for leniency during my work hours. He was fine with it as long as it did not affect my work.

As time passed and the chores of caretaking grew more difficult with time I felt helpless because I had no working knowledge of how to care for a disabled person. And then there were expenses. Much larger than I was prepared to pay. I realized that on day one of her being home, I had to go to fill the medical prescriptions, and buy some medical items for her care. I had to leave her alone that afternoon and hurry to go to the nearest pharmacy. Upon arriving at the pharmacy, and giving the prescription to the pharmacist on duty. He asked me what the payment method would be? I told him I was going to pay cash for it. The Pharmacist told me the price of the medicines, and one of the medications I had to give by injection, which cost me more than a thousand dollars. I asked him, what they were for? And he told me that the medicine was a blood thinner. And that it was one of the most important medications for my wife. The Pharmacist told me that if I did not inject my wife, with that medicine she would suffer another stroke. I said, "I do not have all the money at the moment." The Pharmacist asked me to wait a moment. After a few minutes, he returned and gave me ten injections to be administered to my wife. He also told me that if I did not have money for medicine, and my wife got seriously ill, to call 911. I thanked him graciously. When back home with those ten injections in my hand, I told my wife about what had happened, and she only said that it is God who has worked in the heart of that

Pharmacist. I injected it as instructed, I did not know how to do it, but to both my and my wife's amazement, I did it well. Now I just had to figure out a way to get the money to supply the other medicines. My wife suggested to me to call her brother, to borrow money. I called my wife's brother, and he came to the house that same day. When he arrived, he told me that he only had $300.00. It was gracious of him, but was not enough to acquire all the medication. So in my desperation, I quickly sold my truck for the amount of $2,000.00 even though had I paid $8,000.00 for it. But my wife's life was more important than a vehicle. At that moment it was the wisest decision of my life.

Two days later, I returned to the pharmacy and paid almost $2000.00 for the medicines. The pharmacist seeing me was surprised and shook my hand to greet me. He told me that God had me in his heart, the day he gave me the injections for my wife. And he saw my great anguish and desperation. He said, "May God help you and give you the strength to help your wife." Those words comforted me and gave me strength. After buying the medicine, I returned home, and my wife received me with a smile on her face. I told her that God had already heard our prayers. She was happy and shouted for pleasure "God is great and powerful!" I was already a little calmer, knowing that my wife had her medications.

The days passed, and it was two years later - the recovery of my wife continued slowly. She never recovered from her paralysis; her body remained unresponsive to the physical therapies that the nurses administered her. But my wife never gave up, and she tried to move her body. I understood that the effort she was making was brave.

My moral obligation to my wife was the most important thing of all to me. I was always at her side to support her and take care of her. Out of love and obligation to my wife, I did this for seven years. Through the years I wrote down in a journal what my daily life routine was; Up at 5:00 a.m. every day, to prepare my wife's breakfast, and then help her to eat, because her right hand that she could move trembled so much that it was difficult for her to maneuver a spoon to her mouth. After giving her breakfast, I would help her to use a bedpan in the bed, since she could not walk to the bathroom. I gave her 20-minute massages to help circulate the blood in her body.

Then before I would leave for work, I made sure all her accommodations were accessible on a bedside table where she could reach. I placed a cell phone, the remote control for the T.V., a bottle of water and another with juice. I hated leaving her alone like that, but we could not afford in-home care. I would arrive to work at every day at 7:00 in the morning to my office, where I worked as a property manager. I stayed acutely attentive to my cellphone, in case of an emergency. At 9:00 a.m., I returned to my apartment to tend to my wife's needs.

I would then kiss her on the forehead and said that God and his angels were taking care of her from heaven. She would often cry and tell me that she loved me a lot. I would console her the best I could. I could not accustom myself to seeing my wife in that situation. Then I would go back to my office, where I continued with my work. Although the property was large (200 apartments), the owner never hired an assistant for me. I had to do the job of two people. But it comforted me to know that the owner of the apartments gave me the opportunity to take care of my wife. I always believed that one hand washes the other, and I understood that he was not obliged to help me.

Then at noon each day, on my 1-hour lunch break, I went back to my apartment, to prepare lunch for my wife and I. After eating, I would tend to her personal needs and again head back to work. This was not pleasant for either of us, but it was our reality. God only knows the way in which He enabled me to do it. Allot of the times, she did not enjoy her meals, and it was right then and there that I felt sadness and sentiment towards her. But I had to be strong, and ask God for patience and guidance.

I only had one hour to feed her and myself. And in the last minutes, almost at the hour to return, once again I had to assist my wife to use the bathroom in her bed pan. At 1:00 I would be back at my office. I continued with my work until 3:00 p.m. and again, I had to go back to the apartment to see how my wife was doing and tend her needs. I remember that the first months were the hardest. But with the passage of time and practice, it became easy. I closed my office at 5 o'clock in the evening, and sometimes I had to go to the bank to deposit the rent money. I always took extra care of my driving as to never wanting an accident, because my wife needed me. Oh, how God is so Great and powerful. He always protected me from all danger; I never had an incident or accident.

When I got home, I continued with my task of taking care of my wife, making dinner and cleaning the house. Before going to sleep, I would give her physical therapy; to relax her body and then bathe her. My day ended at 11:00 every night.

What hurt me the deepest was to be away from wife while I worked, I feared what might happen while she was alone. How sad it was for us to live those moments, without anyone who could help. Well, I understood that the responsibility to take care of my wife was mine. As a result of her disability, she should have qualified for Disability, Social Security and Medicare assistance, because this was a humanitarian need, the one thing we needed so desperately. Even though my wife worked in this country for 30 years of her life, she could not qualify for the services or help of the Government. The reason they denied her assistance was because in those days I earned more than $ 2000.00 per month. And that amount excluded her from Government services.

My wife and I believed that this was an injustice, but unfortunately, this is how the system of this Country is structured! I did not know what to do with this situation anymore, the only thing

I did was to pray and ask God for wisdom. I know life seemed very unfair, but I never gave up and did the impossible to help my wife. I want to mention that the owner of the company where I worked, always supported me in my situation. And the only thing I can add is the following; I am deeply grateful to him and his family, God bless him for being such a good person with me, and with all his workers.

So I did this for seven years. God never abandoned me, on the contrary, He conditioned me to my new situation of life. My wife was pleased to have me by her side, and I also enjoyed her company. This shows the importance of falling in love with someone's mind and not their body. I felt that our love was, what gave me strength every day when I woke up. Every morning God renewed me with much energy and good health so I could do what I needed to do each day.

Over time, I came to understand, that it was not easy for my wife or me to accept her medical condition; before her stroke, she was always an active and hard-working woman, and on the weekends she used to help others, she was an earth angel. Now she lay in a bed unable to do anything for herself or anyone else. We were both emotionally affected by this situation. I always tried to give my wife an understanding in this situation. Although we always stayed at the house, I tried to spend the best time with her. We both missed going for walks in the park or visits to California. This new stage of our lives served to bond our relationship even more since we were together all the time.

Our activities changed, now in the afternoon, we read the Bible together. It seems that God united us in that way, she loved that I read the book of Psalms. Little by little I could understand more of the word of God, and I realized that God had a call for me; which was to preach his word and several Christian's in my community persuaded me to follow through with my calling. The Christian group invited me to their Church, and they told me that God had a purpose and a calling for me. But I did not understand what they wanted me to say about that, at first, I thought it was just a joke. I knew that a supernatural force attracted me to read the Bible, but I did not know how to channel that force. With the passage of time, finally, I understood the purpose of God in my life.

That purpose consisted of my spiritual growth, which would serve me to find my salvation and eternal life in the kingdom of God. When God revealed His purpose to me for my life, I dedicate myself fully to reading the Bible, and some other Theological studies. And so it was the way I began to go through my spiritual life. I remember that some Missionaries and Evangelists from different congregations visited me once a week, and they spoke to me about the word of God. The more I listened and read the Bible, the more I understood God's plan. Everywhere I went there was always people evangelizing, and every time, I stopped to listen to them. Even a co-worker, gave me a Bible and recommended that I read the book of Acts.

She told me that I was speaking and acting similar to that of Saul of Tarsus. (St. Paul). She said, "When you finish reading the book of Acts, please call me on the phone." Then I started to meditate and ask myself questions such as, - "Why are so many Christian people telling me the same thing?" Even a co-worker said, "God has a purpose for you in this life." And I, a little skeptical, answered her; "I'm sure you say the same thing to everyone." Every time she spoke to me about the Bible, I asked her if there was any scientific evidence of Faith. She insisted on telling me that no scientific proof was needed; to believe in the success of God, since Faith cannot be measured with scientific instruments. At first, in my arrogance, I did not understand what she was trying to tell me.

The more I talked with that person, the more I could comprehend the Divine things of God. One day she advised me to read the whole Bible, saying, "You can ask God all you need to know, and he will give you all the answers in dreams and visions."

and then added, "Follow all of God's commandments, you will see significant changes in your spiritual, emotional and physical life. Just let God break you and transform you into a new person. And after your brokenness, you will be ready to give your life to Christ." To me, that seemed very complicated, I tried to follow her advice, and started reading the Bible.

During the same month, on Monday morning, she came to my office and told me; "Even if you prove to be a strong person, you have many vulnerabilities like all human beings." Believe me that even with all our faults and errors God loves us.

I was surprised by this person, because she never gave up, even though I responded negatively. Many times I offended her with absurd comments; she took a lot of her valuable time to tell me about the miracles of God. Just to show how charismatic that woman was, God had already done wonders in her life. I can not deny that He existed, through her life experiences... or my own. I had moments of need to talk to God and give myself to Him.

I began to notice the change in myself; God was transforming me. I was already entering a new spiritual plane, a transformation where my body, soul, and spirit were changing; inwardly and outwardly.

Within this spiritual plane, there are no riches, egoism, or evil. Now I was beginning to understand the purpose of my existence. Apparently, this person who spoke to me about the word of God was sent by God to my rescue, and I saw her as an Angel in my spiritual life.

This new experience helped me, to understand my purpose for my wife. Maybe this was the way God would use me, and give my wife peace and tranquility. I concluded that this complete brokenness was the way I would receive God and all He had planned for me. I already felt like a new person, without fear of life or death. My wife could see the change in my behavior towards her, and I gave God the glory, He instilled in me to accept the condition

107

of my wife and be happy; complementing each other. After seeing things this way, I understood that my spouse was a miracle of God. This confession of things relieved my heart and helped me to accept the will of God. At this stage of my life, I understood three different aspects of life. Human beings need the following; Physical therapy, Emotional therapy, and Spiritual therapy.

After I accepted God's plans in my life, I no longer felt alone. Now, God and His Angels helped me take care of my wife. So I spent the days and months together with my wife, waiting for God to give me a sign to be baptized.

I remember that day when Pastor Jaguar-do invited me to become baptized, I answered him with arrogance. I asked for proof of God's existence. I do not know what happened to me. There were moments that I felt the Glory of God in my life and my being. And on the other hand, I questioned His existence. Apparently, my heart had deep wounds, caused by the suffering of the events that I had to live. So many times in my life I thought it was a punishment from God. And I did not understand why I had to give my Life and my Spirit to an unjust God. Would it be for all that I had to live? I did not find a logical answer to my question, and I was still a little confused about the faith. Part of my confusion consisted of my ignorance of the Christian Church. And then secondly was that I did not know what preparation was needed to accept Christ or to be a member of a Church.

To clarify some of my doubts, I asked the Pastor to inspire me and guide me in my Spiritual life. He taught me the fundamental doctrine of the Christian Church. We did not go in-depth of Theology or the things of God. He merely showed me that I needed to be baptized. He also told me that he was ready because God had already sent him the sign that I was waiting for; but that my spiritual state did not allow me to persevere. After he said goodbye that afternoon, I returned home and told my wife what happened. I was thinking about the last thing that those people told me. And with that same thought in my mind, I was busy several days. Trying to find in my mind the signs, but they were not coming to my mind. Until one night a couple of months later, just before going to sleep. I heard a voice inside me, that told me; "Tonight a revelation from God will come to you, an Angel named Ra-suti-el will visit you and bring you to the top of a mountain so that you will be baptized in the fire of the Holy Spirit, and God will engage with you."

And so it happened that the Angel Ra-suti-el came in a dream, and he took me to the mountain, the place where the Angel took me is located in the land of Egypt. And in front of the mountain is a recumbent Lion, similar to the Lion of the tribe of Israel. When we begin to climb the rocky paths of that high hill, I noticed that there was a river pure and crystal clear. I asked the Angel to stop for a moment to see that water. And he said to me, wait until we get to our destination, and you will know where the spring of water is born. I made my way to the location, and I knelt down next to the riverbank, I reached down to splash water on my face, then I drank some of it. That was the purest water that I have ever drunk in my whole life.

When I drank it, I lost my thirst in an instant. The Angel and I continued walking through the valleys of the mountain. And as we got closer, I smelled the scent of sweet roses. And suddenly I felt a very intense heat inside my being. Before reaching the top of the mountain, we took a moment under an olive tree. I sat down on a rock and I looked up in the sky.

Suddenly I noticed that some clouds formed right where I was looking, and suddenly everything was clouded around us. The angel said to me, "Do not fear that the Son of God is coming down from heaven, in that white cloud and light." I turned my eyes upward, to see the son of God descending. I watched in astonishment, and only listened to what the Angel told me. My body remained motionless for a moment, and my feet trembled with emotion. Then we continued walking, and I turned my gaze towards the mountain and then to my surprise I saw that a sea of people were following us. There were thousands of people who were approaching us. They carried trays of food and wine, and some had animals. Finally, upon reaching the top of the mountain, observed two people far in the distance.

One of them was receiving some keys and the One that was standing told him; "Blessed are you, Simon, son of Jonas, because I do not reveal to you my name the flesh or blood, but my Father who is in heaven. And I also tell you, that you are Petra, and on this rock, I will build my Church and I give you at this moment the keys of my kingdom and heaven."(Matt 16-19) And the One who was standing had long hair, and he was dressed in white robe and a purple belt wrapped around his waist. He was also wearing golden sandals, and carrying in his right hand a golden cross-shaped stick, and in his left hand a string of stones of many colors.

I remained immobile and the Angel went to the person who was standing and told him; we are already in front of you, almighty Lord, receive your servant. The son of the True God. And he answered "I am the Lamb of God," his tone of voice was very soft. And with a commanding voice, he said; "I approached my Servant to touch him, so he knows that he is ready to receive my Baptism in the fire." Then the Angel told me; The Son of God wants to touch your body.

I walked with the Angel, and as I approached Jesus Christ I felt that my spirit left my body; and He spoke, "Come with me, do not fear son of man, and do not reject the Kingdom of God to baptize you. You see that great water, that water is born from my body, and it is the same water that comes from the heavens; which forms two rivers within the city of my father God, where two holy lands are formed. The first is the land where the sun is born every day, and it is where the living live. The second land is where the sun is hidden and where the dead dwell. It's part of the end, it's the door to eternity, and that's my domain. 'HEDDEH' IS MY NAME."

He continued to speak, "In this living water I will baptize you, and you will be saved in my name." I approached the water and stood in front of Him. He took my arm and guided me inside the spring of water. He ordered an Angel to put a pitcher in my hands. I took the container in my hands, I filled the pitcher with the water from the running river of pure water. And the Angel stood next to me, then Jesus put his right hand on my head, and slowly submerged me into the living spring; He said the following words, "Today, I have baptized you, in the name of my Father, of his Holy Spirit and in my name Amen" And when he said these things, I saw how a great light in the form of a dove came out from heaven, and I felt the Glory of God descend upon my head, and the Angel embraced me and told me today you have been baptized with fire and the Spirit of God has descended upon you.

And Jesus Christ said with a voice of power, "Look upon man as a son. All those people that have been following you up the mountain have the same spiritual need, and just like you, they need to be baptized, so that when they die, they reach the presence of my father, God. And you will guide them towards The Kingdom of God. You have been chosen, for I give you the keys of Hades, and a pitcher of water, from which a spring of living water is born. Today you will receive a new name, and your new name will be like that of your Angel Ra-suti-el. And everything will be done according to my will, because today you were baptized by me, in the presence of my father God, and of his Holy Spirit."

"I THE SON OF THE TRUE GOD, tell you that in this way of redemption, you will not be alone, my presence and the seven spirits of God will be with you. Just keep in mind; The Baptism is a deed of God. And this mandate must be transmitted from generation to generation, regardless of the age of the people who receive it. What matters is to baptize and save all humanity. Because sin is the same for all, a 5-year-old boy sins and is no different than a man of 100 years; since sin is a human inherited condition, in which its impregnated in every being, and not inherited by their parents; but inherited by God himself.

And before I descended from the mountain, the Son of God invited me to eat with Him. He ordered me to sit on a chair similar to a throne and made me wait a moment. Then he told me; "We will sit at this table, and we will wait for Moses and Elijah. They have light in the form of two fleeting stars, and then we will all sit down together, and in their presence, I will reveal to you how the heavens and the earth were created. And I will also tell you, what the signs of the last days are; and finally, I'll let you know the purpose of my two witnesses. Today we will eat together as four, before the precession of the Spirit of God.

Suddenly there was a trembling noise, and from the heavens, two Lights descended; and between those lights, two people dressed in white. Christ got up from the table, to receive Moses and Elijah. When the three of them greeted each other, I saw how Jesus Christ transformed into pure light, as did Moses and Elijah. And its radiance was too intense for my eyes to I look upon it. Alas, the transformation and the three formed a circle, and I entered inside the circle.

I approached with great fear, and felt a warmth inside my being; my mind became united with theirs, and I joined the prayer that Jesus Christ directed. And as I was praying, flashes of lights and fireballs were seen in the sky when Jesus Christ called out the name of God. And suddenly Moses and Elijah spoke in tongues. But, everything they said, I understood; because we were all one body of light, and the Spirit of God indwelt us.

Jesus Christ, continued with his prayer looking to heaven and said; "Our Father, who are blessed with mercy, do not forsake your servant Jesús, whom I baptized in the company of your Holy Spirit. Protect him from all evil." After the prayer, he said to me. "Now your mission is to rescue souls by baptizing them in The Name of God, Your Name and the name of the Holy Spirit, Amen." After this, we all sat down at the table to share the Lord's sacred Supper. And while we were eating, Jesus Christ took the bread, and blessed it, and broke it, and distributed it saying; "Take, eat; this is my body." And then took the wine, and having given thanks he said. "Drink from it, all of you. This is my blood of the new covenant, which is poured out to many, for the forgiveness of sins" (Matthew 26: 26-28)

After dinner, the three of them said goodbye to me, and I saw how they were getting closer to that white cloud in the shape of a sphere. The sky became wide open, and they disappeared from my sight. A few minutes after His departure, the Angel advised me to rest, because later we would receive all the people who approached the mountain. And rest for a couple of hours in the company of the Angel. And before the night ended a large part of the people had already reached the top of the mountain.

Among the crowd, there were some parents of children who were shouting, "help, help," they were carrying in their arms a dead girl. And they asked me to lay my hands on her, saying; if you are the Son of God, then ask heaven for help. I cried out The Name of God, closed my eyes and I asked my father, God, to send his Spirit to help awaken the girl of that sleep. And I touched her head with my hands, and she woke up, and everyone shouted with pleasure, "The Spirit of God, The son of God is with us" And after that event, the Angel organized all the people to be baptized. That was the will of God, and I started to Baptize all those who came close to me. That night and until dawn, more than a thousand people were baptized, who rejoiced with the power of the Holy Spirit. After this, the Angel said goodbye to me, and I woke up from that intense dream.

When I woke up, I told my wife everything about the dream and how Jesus Christ had baptized me. My wife advised me to call the Pastor, to tell him about my dream. I waited until dawn and called Pastor Jaguar-do. I told him part of my dream on the phone, and he was very interested in knowing more details. That same day he and his family came to my house, I received them with open arms and introduced them to my wife. They were pleased to meet her and then they asked me for the details of my dream. They were amazed as I told them the details of my dream. They said that this was my calling and that Jesus Christ had confirmed it to me that way. It was a very emotional evening. They then invited me to give my testimony in their Church. They told me that my dream was Divine and that it could be used as a message to motivate all of the members. Especially for those who do not yet believe in God, or who are just beginning their journey of faith in Christ.

This time I accepted his invitation and went to his Church, to share my testimony. When the day came to visit his Church, I felt nervous. I did not know how the members of the Church would take it. When I arrived, they were already waiting for me, and they introduced me to the congregation. The Bishop of the church was there and made several comments concerning my dream. I just told him that it was my testimony. He got annoyed by my response and commented, "The fact that you had a dream with Jesus Christ does not make you special." I was polite and waited for the Pastor to call me to the pulpit. When it was my time, I went up there and first I prayed for everyone, and continued with the message that God had revealed to me. During my preaching, I felt that the spirit of God spilled over the congregation and we all cried and praised the Lord. When I finished giving my testimony, I fell to the floor and prayed to God because the Spirit of the Lord was on me.

The brother shepherds dragged me from the floor and helped me get off the altar. They seated me in a chair, and many people in the congregation approached me. They asked me to lay my hands on their heads. I allowed myself to be led by the Holy Spirit, I laid my hands on the sick, and I began to pray for them. And they cried with delight, and they said that they felt the flames of God's spirit. That night with the presence of the Holy Spirit, there were tears, joy, and victory. At the end of the service, I returned home, and I told my wife that I felt the glory of God. And she was happy and congratulated me, she also said to me, "You are already a new person that God has turned you into His pastor, and the seven years of preparation, to meet with God are almost there."

I was thinking about what my wife's message was, the number seven surprised me because in my dream Jesus Christ called the seven spirits that are in front of the throne of God. And seven represents a very powerful kabbalistic number. Many spiritual things are associated with that number. The months went by, and I continued to take care of my wife, and at the same time, I studied the Bible. And in my spare time was also looking for a Church that offers classes in Theology. Asking the people who came to my office, a sister in Christ told me that in the church where she attended also had a Bible Institute. There I spoke with the pastor, I became a member, and I enrolled in the Bible Institute. There was something inside of me that told me to study to be a Pastor.

I thought that it was my calling to be a pastor since my dream had revealed that to me and that I had full support from Jesus Christ, to follow in his footsteps. And just like His mandate is the great commission is to go to all corners of the earth and make disciples, it is also mine. That's what I did together with the co-pastor of the church. I joined the Leader of the council to go out to evangelize a town called Ely Nevada, which was located about 300 miles north from the city of Las Vegas. Also during the week, I evangelized in the parks of Las Vegas. I felt that this is what God wanted from me because the mere fact of talking about God's plans in my life gives me strength. I will always live with gratitude for the things that God has given me and taken away from me. God had already transformed my life, He had manifested in such a clear way in my life that it was impossible for me to deny his existence.

These spiritual experiences together with my wife, helped us to understand the grace of God, and made us grow spiritually. I felt inside my heart, a deep love for my wife, so much love that I will never forget. We both needed each other; she needed care and I needed tranquility in my life. My new attitude towards life new and exciting, God finally finished his work in me. Everything was going well in my life and with my wife, Sue. For a while, we did not think about her illness, until one day she felt bad, and ended up in the Emergency room. She complained of a bad headache. Her head had swollen on the right side, it looked like it was going to explode.

When she was admitted to the Hospital, the Doctors did a Tomography report. My wife was there for two weeks. The Neurologist ordered a small surgery called "Shunt Procedure." but the recovery was so slow that she ended up in a place of Rehabilitation. She could not return home because of her health condition. Now she required observation 24 hours a day. For me, it was very painful to see her in that condition. I remember that sometimes she no longer made sense of what she was talking about. I am sure this was very hard on her too.

Her recovery was slow and she was there for a year, and I visited her every day that was the saddest of all my years. I encouraged by telling her that very soon I was going to take her home. This was difficult for both of us because we both needed each other. Sometimes she would become distraught saying; "You sent me to this place for old people." But she did not understand that her state of health required professional care 24 hours a day. She could not comprehend how much I was hurting not being able to have her come home. I couldn't make her understand that I would never abandon her. And a lot of the times I would confess that my soul breaks every single day seeing her in that situation, but couldn't find the words to say it. We both accepted the situation and let life take its course.

She locked herself in that lonely place and I at home looking for what to do to keep my mind occupied. To distract my mind and not think so much about my wife's illness, I enrolled in another semester at Bible Institute to continue with my studies to be a Pastor.

At the end of the first year of study at the Institute, I noticed that my personality was changing and I did not carry things with pessimism. Now I understood more about my existence and my relationship with God. This new way of seeing life made me give myself entirely to the Church of God. I will not lie to you when I say that my preparation in the Institute was easy, on the contrary, it was days of hard study, fasting, and prayer; but, since I learned to have self-control of my Mind, Body, and Soul. My spirituality had grown so much that I did not recognize myself. Some of my friends criticized me for my change. But it brought tranquility to our lives. It was good for both me and my wife.

And I would like to speculate saying, that maybe it will also help you in your spiritual development. I remember one day while visiting my wife; I told her that I had had a Divine vision, in which God urged me to go up to pray on a mountain. And in that vision, he revealed something to me. "To go to the top of Mount Charleston, and when you get there, I will prepare you for your Priesthood, and after your ordination, you will serve as a Pastor for eternity." I replied saying, "I'll do as you say and I'll be cautious."

During the first week of June 2015, I was waiting for another sign from God. And God came again in a Devine vision and told me; "The day has come for you to go up to the mountain." Before going up to the mountain, I prepared for three days and three nights, fasting and praying. When the day arrived, I went to visit my wife, and I brought her a bouquet of red roses. I said goodbye to her as if it were my last day of life, and I gave her lots of hugs and kisses, we also talked about a few of our great memories when we camped in the mountains. At the end of that day and after a great conversation, she understood that what I was doing was not bad, but on the contrary, everything was part of our spiritual growth.

I said goodbye to her with a hug and a kiss and returned home. When I entered my apartment, I went into the living room and asked God for wisdom. After awhile, I began to pack some things, and I got ready to leave for the mountain. I put my Bible inside my backpack; also add clothes and provisions, along with a couple of blankets. I took everything to my vehicle and started the trip, before leaving the city I went through a gas station to fill the fuel tank. I was ready to leave the city and heading to the mountain, I turned on my stereo and listened to a CD of praise to raise my spirit. The road was lonely, with hardly another car on it. The night and you could see the sky full of stars. I asked God to guide me, and that it was he who pointed me to the place, where he wanted to see me. I drove for more than 40 minutes, and immediately a White Donkey was on the road. I stopped to let him cross but he walked very slowly. I backed off the road and got off to wait for the Donkey to move, and when I looked up I got a surprise, it was not just one Donkey but seven in all. I just smiled and said; here is the place where God wants to talk to me, that was the sign that I was looking for.

I parked the truck on the side of the road, grabbed my Bible with a blanket and my backpack with provisions. I started to climb up the narrow mountain roads, as I climbed to the top thoughts of the early Church came to my mind, I imagined that God thus communicated with our ancestors, and exhorted them to have an encounter with him in the mountains, Moses is the best example, according to the scriptures of Exodus. Comforting myself, my heart was exalted with emotion and throbbed very quickly. Maybe it was because of the excitement of knowing that at any moment I would meet God.

I also felt impure when I thought that it was only seven days of fasting and prayer, and I felt that my body had not purified in its totality, but I assumed that God would cleanse the impurities of my mind, body, and soul. As I was deepening along the dark paths, I saw a part of the mountain, which was shaped like a lamb, representing the body of the heir of the kingdom of God. "HED-DEH!" I exclaimed. And after exclaiming his name "My God, my God" I saw a flat and open space, I stopped to contemplate the sky, and from that place, I could observe a significant part of the stars of the sky.

At Las Vegas Nevada; Charleston Mountain at sunrise

And walk on that spot, and then I reached an altar made of fine gold, and in front of that altar was an Angel dressed in white, sitting on a rock, and The Angel had a golden staff in his right hand, and with his left hand he fired shot towards the ground, to purify the earth where I was walking. When he felt my presence, He moved towards me, looked me in the eyes, and with a voice of thunder told me this way: "I am your Guardian Angel, and I am the one who leads you to the presence of God." And suddenly a light appeared and I noticed that there was another Angel standing next to an Eagle, which was spreading its wings preparing to fly and the Eagle flew over the heavens and disappeared in the sky.

119

The name of the second Angel is Aseb-Edo, and he told me that he came from Neser-eno-Sert. This means, "Nazarene of Galilee." And the Angel ordered me to look to the west of the sky because from there I would see a signal of fire. And in that place, I stayed paralyzed and called the name of God to the four winds. And as I cried out the name of God, a Voice within my being told me this way; "Look up to the sky and look at the stars because that is my sacred mantle covered by Stars, Planets, Comets, and Galaxies."

I continued with my prayers and exclaimed the name of God, then I felt a slight breeze with water hitting my body and saw how the sky covered with clouds, which gave me the impression that they were formed out of nothing. And I asked God for a sign of His presence, and God answered saying, "You see the clouds in the sky, that same cloud was the one that led Moses through the desert of Egypt, when he escaped from Pharaoh." Then, a third Angel was revealed to me, and that angel was sitting on a square stone, with a golden staff in his hands, and a sun on his head, which illuminated his body. And in front of him a clay pot full of water. And on one side of it, there was a pond of pure, crystal clear water. And the name of the Angel is Mu-o-Ses, This angel spoke with me and said; "God manifests himself in front of his people and also in front of his servants in different ways, but his people are distracted in their slums and sins. And His servants are confused among their false doctrines, written by their false Prophets, who lack a presence of His Spirit and revelation. And now they have my people in limbo from hell" He continued saying, "This is the message I bring you; God has trained you with intelligence and wisdom and gave you the gift of a Prophet, so you interpret their messages, dreams and signals manifested through their natural elements. Especially in the four natural elements; water, fire, air, and earth, because these elements are the essence of all things in the universe." And when the Angel finished telling me these things, the sky turned purple and there was a large golden door, and as it opened up with a loud deafening sound, and fire bolts started to come out from between the door, and those balls of fire crossed the skies and descended on the face of the earth, and burned a part of the mountain. And after a moment of a rain of fire, the sky cleared up and all the stars were seen again.

The Angel sitting on the Golden stone announced himself to be Aseb-Bedo. And I continued laying on the ground prostrated praying, asking God for wisdom and understanding. Then God spoke saying, "My son, you are a brave man asking me to prove my existence, that makes you a unique child among all the humans of these times and of these generations, I will give you wisdom and understanding in accordance with my Prophets, and I God "HED-DEH" I will give you the Gift and the power of my Spirit so that you are a Prophet.

I will provide you with knowledge about all the things of my kingdom, and also I will give you the keys of my hidden places for humanity and with the keys, you can open and close the doors of eternity." And I asked him for another sign, and God manifested again. And a fourth Angel appeared in front of me and told me; "Look at the ground, that floor on which you find yourself is sacred. Take off your shoes and put on these golden sandals, so you do not contaminate part of the altar of the Lord." And I did as the Angel instructed and put on the golden sandals, and I continued praying, and the Angel joined my prayer. Suddenly there was a great whirlwind, my eyes and my mouth were filled with dust, The Angel covered me with his Wings, and the wind ceased.

The name of the fourth Angel is Seb-Astian, he was kneeling on the ground and with his finger drawing a spiral on the ground that formed a rock from the sand he was twirling, and he supernaturally instilled the part of God's Spirit into it, and when he was finished, he gave me that rock, and he told me that that was another sign from God. And he ordered me to protect that rock, and to take care of it with my life; because that is the rock that will be used as a symbol, for the construction of God's New Kingdom. And everyone who touches that rock will be saved from all sin and will pass to eternal life without knowing death. And the quickly the Angel stood up, to scare away a Swan that approached the sacred place. And I asked him, "What does the presence of that bird mean in this holy place, and why does he have two eggs with him?"

He answered, "Here was the place where the Gods children were born that one day they may inhabit the earth." And my spirit was filled with joy when I heard the words of the Angel, and that is how God manifested that night. I was shown the mysteries of the creation of Adam and Eve, like particles of dust and dirt embedded in stone with the body of a man and a woman.

I continued to pray and I cried out again the name of God and asked Him to transform me into a new person. And a fifth Angel appeared, this angel ordered me to turn my gaze to where the sun rises, so that I could feel the Glory of God. And when I turned my face to the East, I felt a hand touch my cheek, and that hand opened my mouth, and then I felt warm breath blow down inside my being. And that hand was the most subtle and delicate hand I had ever felt. And I heard the sound of the wind, as it approached the mountain. And the Angel that accompanied me had a cross in his right hand, and in his left hand a white and red striped flag, with thirteen stars on it, and I asked the Angel, "What is the meaning of this flag?" And he simply said, "It is a flag that will mark the land, of the people promised by God to His children, and the breath of God will give life to a new nation, and His flag will always remain firm and in motion." And the name of the Fifth Angel is Nefu-Ra."

After this last signal the five Angels formed a circle around me and joined in my prayers, and in heaven there was a golden door, which was guarded by four Cherubim and on the other side of the door, I saw a Being sitting on a throne of gold, and his body shone like burnished gold. In His right hand, He was holding a measuring rod. And in His left hand, He had a string with stones of many colors. And then he said in a voice of loud thunder; "You are my Servant, and you will be the Prophet of my new people, who will be the foundation of my new Church; in the land promised to your ancestors." And I also tell you, "That you were my servant, since that day when my son baptized you on the mountain. That was the day when my spirit descended upon you. At that moment, I gave you the power, to govern over earthly and heavenly waters, and I also gave you the keys to the doors of my kingdom, which extends to eternity."

And then he said, "When you enter my Heavenly Kingdom, you will sit to my right, and you will live with my Son Jesus Christ for eternity, and I will give you a new home. This will be the new era for humanity. And this house is represented by a woman with the appearance of a Virgin, and that Virgin carries in her hands a pitcher. And from that pitcher come heavenly seas of water. But now is not the time that I reveal all the things of my throne, for now, go back to your house and with your people who are thirsty to know my mysteries. And patiently wait for my last signal which will reach you through my Angels. And they will reveal the details of our last meeting. And after that meeting, your spirit will shine like a Star in the sky. And your brightness will be brighter, than the Morning Star." Amen...

After listening to the words of God, I said goodbye to the Angels and descended from the mountain. And the Angles rejoiced at the wonders that God revealed to me, and they said; "Go back to your people and tell them the revelations of God. Also visit your wife, because she is expected to hear about your experience on the mountain and tell her the good news." And as I was coming down off the mountain, my body was indwelt with the Holy Spirit, and I felt a heat flowing through my body. And through that heat, I received the healing of God, and my mind was purified from all evil thoughts and my body no longer lived with all its evils.

I arrived at my house and rested for half a day, and then went to visit my wife. And I told her all the wonders that I witnessed on the mountain, and she said, "God is preparing you to exercise your priesthood, and you found your true Church on earth. Which will not be contaminated by false Doctrines, written by false Prophets, Apostles or Theologians; Which their names does not exist among the list of Prophets and Apostles of the holy books of God. Those false worldly Doctrines were pressed upon the people of God; by orders of Governments or Religious entities. Which have kept the human spirit captive, in ignorance and sin."

I respected my wife, and I agreed with her, and I said, "I know that the people of God have been deceived, and entangled among those absurd ideologies, which lack the Divine revelation of God. But you know something Sue, we should not judge them, because, like them, we are all imperfect people full of sin." After that conversation with my wife, I prayed for her. And during the prayer session, I transmitted the heat of my body to my wife, and she felt it, and I felt that energy healed her inside. I touched her head and told her that it was God who was healing her, that I was just an instrument used by God. And after I said those words, she fell silent in a deep sleep, I said goodbye to her giving her a kiss on her forehead.

I returned home to rest, I felt exhausted. When I arrived at my house I sank into the lounge chair and I fell asleep. I was so fatigued that I slept like a rock and woke up until the next morning. I can say that the heat that my body emanated had remained in me for a whole week. During that week I went to talk to my Pastor and tell him what happened. He said to me: "I can't believe what you're telling me, because God does not manifest himself to humans in that way, and furthermore not to a common person as yourself." That was the condemnation of my Pastor, so I respectfully listened and then I said, "I challenge you in your prayers, to ask God for a sign as proof of His existence, and I hope God will answer your

124

prayers, and when that happens, I hope that God Himself will encourage you to climb a mountain alone. And so you will have that opportunity, to ask God why He chose me to give this message. But as I know, you lack that courage that is required to talk to God; I don't care about your opinion."

After talking with the Pastor, I stayed in the Church to pray alone, and ask God for understanding, and above all for humility. I did not understand why the Pastor offended me in that way but think that all human beings are full of imperfections, and racial hatred among ourselves. I decided not to tell anyone else what I lived on the mountain, but write it and do the will of God. I continued with my normal life and continued taking my pastorate classes at the Bible Institute, I wanted to graduate to obtain my Pastor Certification, and thus be able to preach in some Church. While I was finishing my studies, I congregated in a small church in the city of Las Vegas. And in my free time, I offered a Bible Study in my apartment, some of my neighbors responded to my invitation. And some others criticized me because they said that I didn't have a Pastor certificate.

At Las Vegas Nevada; Church Event at Pecos Apartments

I put aside the criticism of the people, and let God guide me and strengthen me. I was not going to allow the negative comments to stop me from my calling or cause me to lose any sleep. This event of discord among my neighbors, made me reflect on the natural essence of man, and the spiritual struggle between good and evil, I concluded that the heart of man is conflictive by nature and that behavior keeps him in a primitive mental state. After meditating on these things, I thanked God for His help in my life. And humbly continued with my Spiritual mission, thanks to my humility I could pay more attention to the people, who really needed to hear the word of God, I understood that the group of nonconformists, was only a reflection of those who are of God, or they are simply embedded in false Doctrines that they do not understand.

"Ultimately, salvation is individual." And God teaches us with a free Spirit, which can discern between good and evil. Positive thinking changed my personality, and this state of mind made me pay more attention to my spiritual needs. I also understood that my spirit belongs to God, and He will one day take it back, and when that day comes, I will be prepared, so as not to feel death. Again I went to visit my wife and told her about my activities with holding Bible studies in my apartment and also told her that every time I organized an event, discords broke out between my neighbors.

She only answered me; "The behavior of human beings is very complicated since many of us have our own criteria." She encouraged me to continue my work in my community, but I noticed a sense of sadness in her soul. And I asked, why so sad?" She quietly answered with her voice cracking, "I feel very proud of you, but I feel a great pity being a hindrance to you." I looked her in the eyes, and I saw her eyes spill a couple of tears, I embraced her and told her to forget about that thought. That she was very important in my life and that I needed her by my side. But she continued crying, and her emotions made her talk without thinking.

Again she told me that she would rather die so that I would be free and fly high.

I asked her to change the conversation because those thoughts were very sad, but she continued with the same discussion. She finally said, "My headaches are getting stronger every time, and I'm afraid to sleep. Because I felt that when I closed my eyes, I would not wake up again." After listening to her, I was speechless and asked her not to feel that way. She shed a few tears and closed her eyes. I just hugged her and asked her to accept Jesus Christ as her only Savior. After a while, she fell asleep, and I went home. I left thinking about what my wife had told me. I noticed she seemed a little confused in her thoughts, she spoke in pauses and she left the topics in mid-sentence. That worried me and I decided to return the next day very early. When I arrived at the rehabilitation center, it was July 2, 2016, a Saturday. Everything seemed normal, I went with my wife to eat, she ate very little, she told me that she was not hungry; she wanted to sleep because she was tired.

I told her to sleep for a while, and I would stay be by her side! She closed her eyes and fell asleep. After a few hours, I said goodbye to her; I told her I was going to let her rest. She opened her eyes and said goodbye to me, told me to come back the next day to talk about her dreams, I told her; "Of course, tomorrow I will see you." I decided to return home, but I got, worried, something inside felt wrong. I got home and the hours passed and I was still worried about my wife's health. I could not sleep all night, several times I went out to walk around the property, suddenly, I saw that a wolf walked by me, I thought it was a domesticated dog at first. But some of my neighbors alerted me to the danger that I walked into; they told me he was a wolf, and that he had attacked one of his dogs.

Thinking that the wolf is thirsty and hungry, I gave him water and meat. The hours of dawn passed, and the wolf did not leave, I returned to open the door of my apartment, and the moment I opened the door the wolf quickly came inside. I tried to take it out but I could not, he went to the bedroom and climbed into my wife's bed, he stayed for a while, and then left. I did not understand what was happening; I thought it was a dream. It was 6:00 in the morning and I could not sleep. The sun came out and I made coffee with bread, tried to sleep again, closed my eyes and fell asleep. At 8:00 am my phone rang, and I answered it quickly, I heard the sharp voice of a young lady; I asked her who she was, she told me she was a nurse for my wife, at TLC Care Center. The nurse informed me that my wife could not wake up; they examined her earlier that morning, and she was fine. The nurses added, "We do not know what happened to her, but now her breathing is very slow, and her skin was purple" I only said; "I'll be there in 15 minutes." I dropped the phone and dashed to my truck.

My mind was elsewhere, I wanted to arrive in a moment. Before leaving the apartment, one of my neighbors told me how to get there a little faster. I told him that my wife was in serious condition and he told me how sorry he was. I headed towards the periphery and took Interstate 515 South. That day there wasn't much traffic on the road, which helped me to get there faster. While driving, I turned on the radio, and as things of destiny, the DJ was playing one of my wife's favorite songs, "Los Bukis" (Si teamotanto). Paying attention to the song, I got lost in its lyrics, singing along with so much feeling and pain, that it made me forget the notion of time and space. I accelerated my car; I wanted to arrive NOW. But after the song, I realized I needed to slow down. I decided I better arrive alive, and being late was better than never.

Before exiting the freeway, I saw a traffic accident; an 18-wheeled truck crashed into a red sports car. I just shook my head in horror and kept driving, when I got to the TLC Rehabilitation Center, I parked and got out and quickly headed inside and registered, then ran through the corridors to get to my wife's room. When I entered her room, I found her unconscious. It seemed that she was in a deep sleep, I said, "Sue, wake up, I am here, Sue wake up! She moaned in pain. I kept calling her, I took her by the hand, and I noticed that the nails of her fingers and her lips were purple. I took my Bible in my hands, I closed my eyes and began to pray aloud, I thought that maybe when listening to my prayers she would wake up. I called the nurses into the room, I asked: "what is the condition of my wife?" The nurse brought my wife's file and showed me a document that my wife had done a few months ago. It said, that my wife did not want to be resuscitated, or administered first aid. The people were only respecting that document since that was the last will of my wife.

I asked them to leave me alone with my wife, and the nurses left the room. I continued with my prayers, and I asked God for a miracle, I said: "Lord give me the opportunity to say goodbye to my wife, I know that she listens to me, and I know that you have the power to grant me this miracle." Nothing caused me to cease my request, and continued praying and I cried out the name of God. I stayed for more than an hour without stopping. I almost gave up, seeing that my wife did not respond. But as a last resort to awaken her, I mentioned the name of God "HED-DEH" in her ear, and she heard me, she reacted by moving her hands. And heard her voice saying: "Where are you honey? I can't see you!" She extended her arms to touch my face, but she lost her sense of sight. She asked me to turn the light on because she saw everything dark, she felt my face, and I told her to calm down. I said: "I am already here by your side, and God accompanies us." I took her in my arms, and I sat her up on the bed, I kissed her on the forehead, and I told her to take a deep breath.

She followed my instructions, and little by little began to breathe better, after a little while, she recovered completely. And her sight was renewed, but she told me that she had a sharp pain in her brain. I asked her to be checked out by a Doctor, but her voice was shallow, and she said "I'm tired of living in this condition, with so many body pains, and it's almost eight years, and I'm not getting better, on the contrary, I'm getting worse every day. My body is deteriorating along with my spirit, which already wants to escape to be free in eternal life." But I begged her to go to the specialists. Also to give an opportunity for her daughter and her grandchildren to see her. When I mentioned the name of her grandchildren, she told me to call the ambulance, and that later she would contact her daughter. I ran out into the hall and said the nurse that my wife had woken up; that she wanted to go to the hospital.

The nurses called an ambulance, I returned to my wife's room, and told her that the ambulance was already on the way. She asked me about her daughter, and I said to her that I would inform her of the situation. I took her by the hand and told her that I loved her alot and that it hurt me so much to see her suffer. She just smiled and asked me; "What do you want to do in this life?" I did not know what to answer; I just focused on keeping her awake to take her to the hospital. When the paramedics arrived, they told me to leave the room and wait. They had to prepare her to transport her to the nearest hospital.

It took about twenty minutes to load her into the ambulance, and they gave me the address of the hospital. She would be hospitalized. I decided that I would follow them so as not to get lost. We left the parking lot and headed to the east side of the city, and it took us about fifteen minutes to get to the Hospital (St. Rose de Lima Hospital). I parked and went to the emergency room, I registered and they told me that they would call me when my wife was registered I waited more than thirty minutes. At last, when they called me, they told me where she was.

The receptionist gave me access to the Emergency area, she took me to my wife's room. When she saw me she smiled and asked me; "Why did you take so long? I replied; "It is the protocol to follow." I took a chair and sat next to her, I tried to reassure her because I was very nervous. She told me that she would not let them harm her or do any surgery on her anymore. I told her that I was going to stay to protect her and she hugged me and kissed me on my cheek. I corresponded with a kiss on her forehead, and suddenly she started coughing and could not breathe, this alerted the nurses, and they tried to put an oxygen mask on her, and she rejected it, she pulled it off and said that it was useless because it was already her last moments. She asked us to let her die, that God already wanted to take her to reunite her with her mother.

The nurse told her it was for her own good, but my wife complained of severe headaches, and could not sedate her because her oxygen level was very low, in the first blood studies, she concluded that the CO_2 level, in her blood was three times higher than average. And the doctors had to act quickly to save her life. The doctor talked to me and told me that he had something to do to reduce the level of carbon dioxide. "We only have fifteen minutes to act; you need to talk to your wife." At first, when I spoke to her, she was insisting on letting her die, but after a few minutes, she decided she would do the procedure. Before the Nurse arrived, my wife asked me to pray for her and to read her the Bible "St. Matthew" in particular, and the book of Psalms." I took my Bible and began to look for the book of Psalms. She told me that she wanted to listen to Matthew first; since that was the book she liked the most.

I followed my wife's instructions, and I began reading the book of St. Matthew, and suddenly she told me that she felt the presence of Jesus Christ, she said that He was standing next to her, He asked her to accept Him before leaving since her soul was precious to Him. She told me that with a little water to baptize her because that was the will of God. I went looking for a bottle of water and when I returned to the room, my wife said that Jesus Christ was taking her hand and that He was revealing the wonders of His Kingdom. I took a picture with my cell phone at that moment, to have it as a memory of her Baptism. She started talking very slowly saying that Jesus Christ was caressing her on her forehead and saying, "You are a blessed woman because on your deathbed you have believed in me, now your Soul belongs to me."

And Jesus said goodbye to my wife, also told her before I leave I will give life to a person in this room; and in the distance in one of the rooms, the medical team tried to resuscitate a person, administering mouth to mouth resuscitation. The efforts of the nurses, compressing the patient's chest, the person did not respond

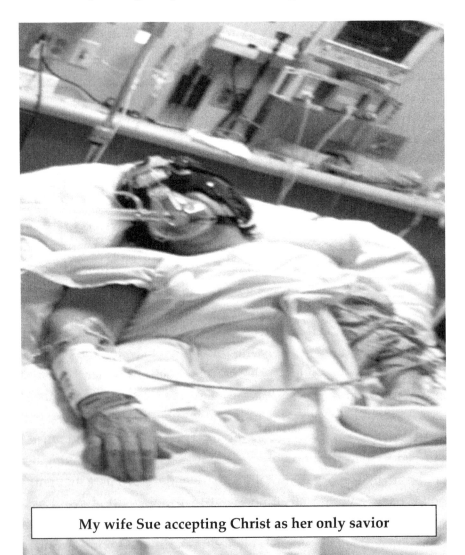

My wife Sue accepting Christ as her only savior

to attempts to resuscitate. Suddenly my wife said; Jesus Christ is on his way to the room of that patient, he says, "I will resuscitate him, he is only asleep, and I am coming back." And suddenly we heard many cries of happiness; the patient had resuscitated. We all applauded and shouted at the same time "God is here with us." Amen ...

After everything had happened it went silent, and my wife told me, Jesus Christ is gone, He just said goodbye to me. And I'm in charge of telling you so; "I will always be with your husband, until the time of his death, he has proven to be a good man." Those years that you have taken care of me were the basis and your preparation in your spiritual life.

Suddenly a man dressed in white entered the room, but clothing was different from that of the Doctors or Nurses. He told me that he would take my wife to the X-ray room, and then they would take a CT-scan of her Skull. On the way to the X-Ray room, the young man who was pushing my wife's stretcher said to us: "I have not seen you since August 20, 2008. That was the day Sue was in the Sunrise Hospital for the first time. He told her, "I was that young man who pushed the stretcher to take you to the surgery room, with your Neurologist Scott Selco" My wife remembered him somehow and said, "Your name is "EDDE" right?" He answered, "Yes, that's my name." It was so amazing; I wanted to get a picture of him with my wife. He said I could take the photo.

We continued with the conversation; He said: "You know, Sue, that Doctor Selco is still working as a neurologist. And now he works in this hospital, with good luck he will be your Doctor."

After the X-rays and the CT scan, the young man returned my wife to her room. The Doctor from the Emergency station said; "As soon as I receive Sue's results, I'll send her to a specialist." After about thirty minutes, the results came into the hands of the Doctor, and they transferred my wife to intensive care. Immediately they started the treatment, to counteract the levels of Carbon Dioxide in her blood. And the hours passed slowly, waiting for my wife to recover. After half a day, my wife's daughter arrived at the hospital. As soon as she entered the room, she shouted loudly, "Mama," I told her to calm down that her mother was in an induced coma. She got angry, took her hand and started talking to her.

I left the room to give her a moment alone with her mother, and I went to the cafeteria to eat a sandwich. Upon returning from the cafeteria, my stepdaughter told me that the Specialist saw her mother. She also told me that The Doctor recognized her mother, from the Sunrise hospital. She gave me the Doctor's card and to my surprise, it was Dr. Selco. Quickly I ran to the nurses' station and asked when would be the next visit of Dr. Selco? They told me that the next day, 11:00 am. I wrote it down on a piece of paper so it would not forget, I went back to the room and said goodbye, and I told them that I would return tomorrow at 10:00 am. I kissed my wife on the forehead and left the room, I returned home to get some sleep.

On the way home, I analyzed everything that was happening in the Hospital and concluded that the miracles of God were beginning to manifest. I did not find a logical explanation, nor did I understand how the same Doctor, who attended my wife years ago was the same Doctor again at a different Hospital. Only God makes events like this possible, and we humans do not understand His mysteries. I only asked God for wisdom to understand life, and I left all control to Him. I thought I could not do anything, to improve the situation of my wife. When I got home, I read the Bible and read the book of Kings, then prayed before going to sleep. I could not get to sleep all night, I just had thoughts of my wife, and I wanted to talk to Dr. Selco. I wanted to ask him to do a miracle, and that with a good medical treatment; he would save my wife's life.

Finally, after a couple more hours of praying, I was able to sleep. The next day I woke up very early, had a light bite to eat, and I went to the Hospital, I took the shortest route to get there faster, but as always the unexpected. There was a car accident on the road, so I was forced to take another route. It would seem that God was sending me signals to control my anxiety and desperation by coming to the Hospital. Finally, I arrived at my destination and it was 11:05 in the morning, I parked as fast as I could, and ran to my wife's room. Upon entering my wife's room, I greeted her but she was in a deep sleep. I sat next to her and took my Bible in my hands to pray for her.

Suddenly a person entered the room, and he recognized me instantly, mentioned my name and told me that he was Dr. Selco. I could not believe he was the same neurologist who had done the first surgery on my wife. I greeted him by the hand, and he looked me in the eyes, told me that everything would be fine. Tears came, and I told him that I needed a miracle. He told me that he could not make a miracle happen, because of my wife's condition. "God does Miracles and God himself knows when to take people home." I was speechless. He told me that they could not do anything for my wife anymore. Sue opened her eyes when she heard him say those words, and she made a sign with her hand, saying that she wanted to die.

Before the Doctor left the room, I told him that his assistant "EDDE" had transferred my wife from the Emergency room to that room. And he told me it was impossible, I told him that I had taken a picture of him and he told me to show it. Take my phone and look in the photo gallery that photo of "EDDE", and when I showed him the photo of EDDE, we were both surprised because EDDE did not appear in the photo everything went blurry.

Dr. Selco told me, it cannot be possible because EddE had died a year ago. I told him that he had told me that he was working with him from Sunrise Hospital and that he had transferred to ST. Rose Delima along with him. He said that it was true but that "EDDE" was already dead. My wife told me that EDDE was an Angel of God and that he was with her all the first day of her hospitalization.

135

After that conversation, Dr. Selco said goodbye to us, after he left the room my wife miraculously became alert and wrote on a piece of paper that said to disconnect the artificial ventilator machine. She wanted to talk to her daughter and me. I told her that it was hazardous to disconnect because she could not breathe and might die, but she insisted so much that I called the Doctors and showed them the paper in which my wife had written her request. They told me to give them some time to organize everything, and they said to me that in two hours it might be possible. For the time being, I was sitting next to my wife, and I took her by the hand and told her that everything would be fine. In her eyes you could see the pain she had, her eyes were sad and her eyes full of tears. I did not ask to see her suffer; I asked God to do his will. I continued with my prayers, and a while later, the nurses came in and told me that the doctors were on their way to remove the breathing tube. She ordered me to leave the room and return in thirty minutes.

I left the room and headed to the cafeteria to get some coffee and then I took my coffee and went through the double doors to a garden area. I sat on one of the benches and looked around. I listened to the singing of the birds, the buzzing of bees. My mind absorbed everything that happened around me, I fixed my eyes to the sky, and I saw how it was cloudy. They were dark clouds and then it started to rain a little. It was a silent moment of reflection and tranquility for me, as I watched the raindrops gently hit the windows and run down the sides. After thirty minutes I returned to my wife's room. When I entered the room, she was awake and she had a hard time breathing. But she could speak clearly and said, "Hello my love how are you?" I ran to her and hugged her, I told her I was fine. I asked her how she felt? She told me that he was very tired and sleepy. Every time she breathed phlegm would come up through her mouth.

I was alarmed, and I called the nurse to ask if that was normal. The nurse told me yes because her trachea was irritated. When the nurse came out of the room, my wife asked me to call her daughter and her brother; because she wanted to say goodbye to them. I took my phone and called her relatives; they told me that they were on their way to the hospital.

While awaiting the arrival of my brother-in-law, my wife told me that she already felt death. I asked her "What would you like me to do for you?" She replied, "Live your normal life and fulfill your call to be a Pastor, and finally cremate my body. And when you cremate me, divide my ashes into three parts. One part is for my cousin Glicina, the second part to my daughter, and the third part to you. And this is what I want you to do with my ashes; Glicina will give her part to my cousin who lives in Texas, and put the urn in the room where they have all our family members who have died. To my daughter Mariel, you tell her that she gives me a little service, in the company of my grandchildren since she did not bring them to see me.

After the ceremony that she throws my ashes into a river. Because my spiritual guide was the Angel that represents the living Water of a spring. And finally, the remains you will place the ashes inside four urns in the shape of a heart, and you will go up to the mountain where God guides you, and that mountain is part of the land of the Hittites, the same land where you found your healing a few weeks ago. And the Angels of God will take you in vision in that holy place. When you pray for my eternal life, you will also pray for all of humanity. Then spread my ashes to the four winds and they will fall on the earth, which will give life to the vegetation. That is my last will." I cried when I heard the decision of my wife, I never thought I would hear her talk like that. I felt a lump in my throat and I could not speak, and she continued speaking: "Thank you for everything, my love, God will compensate you for everything you have done for me."

I would like you to never forget me, and that you always have me in your mind; since where I am going, it is a sacred place, and from heaven, I will take care of you I will be like a guardian Angel to you. Thanks again for all the years that you took care of me, without giving up and above all, thank you because you never left me. I already talked to God, and I asked may He be the one to compensate you for being such a good husband. He will give you wisdom and Intelligence and He will prepare you for your Priesthood on earth. You will deliver this message to the nations: The new Jerusalem has already been founded. And the new era brings in his hands a pitcher of water. Well at last, that day that you will spread my ashes, you will have your third encounter with God, He will reveal all the things you have always wanted to know.

And that will be your last encounter with God, and you will become an Angel of light, like a Star in the firmament, and you will be like the shining Morning Star." Those were part of my wife's last words. And again she asked us to let her go; she touched her head and said she could not stand the pain. And when my wife finished speaking, I called the nurses to let them know what my wife's will was. The nurses understood the situation and told me that I would have to transfer her to a Hospice Care. As my wife was aware, she herself signed all the necessary documents for that process.

I felt defeated, and I did not know what to do. The one thing I did was resign myself and respect my wife's will. But I wanted to be in my wife's place, and have sacrificed my life for her. So that she could enjoy her grandchildren, but the reality was different. After the doctors authorized her transfer, the paramedics arranged to escort her to an ambulance. I asked if I could accompany my wife, and they said yes. I got in the ambulance along with my wife, I held her hand, for a moment, my mind was disrupted with thoughts of the happiest moments of our life together. I felt the speed of Ambulance throughout my body, as if my mind had merged with all matter. I wanted time to stop forever, so as not to reach the place where my wife was going to go to live a better life. There were so many memories that I did not know which was the most beautiful and painful of all, maybe all the moments were beautiful for her and me.

I felt that I was living something surreal, and I was wondering in silence. "What will my wife feel? What will happen to her mind, to know you are at your last moments of life? To distract my mind, I turned my eyes out the ambulance window. The night was sad there was no moon, and the lights of the city dimmed the brightness of the stars. As we approached the final destination, my heart was beating faster. I took my wife by the hand and asked her. Do you recognize the streets? She answered yes I do recognized one of the buildings. I asked her, "Do you know where we are?" and she looked me in the eyes and told me; "I know these streets, we are on Flamingo Avenue and that is the street of the place where we met, Golden Pond Apartments."

I wondered how will she remember us, and I told her that moment was always in my mind. When she heard those words, she shook out her hand and made a circle with her finger, and told me "Look what life is. My life cycle is about to close." When she said that I felt a big lump in my throat and began to weep.

I never thought I would live such difficult moments. And much less I thought that one day I would see a loved one die. With great pain in my heart, I can say; that life does not prepare us for those moments. God sends Angels of light, for our spiritual growth and to make our path lighter.

When arriving at our destination, I felt in my body, a chill that ran from the tip of my feet to my head. When the doors of the Ambulance opened, I let my wife go, and I told her that I had no way of forgetting. She smiled and told me "You have to be strong and follow your life path; I'm going to a better place. And in that place, I'll be waiting for you..." The paramedics interrupted our conversation and ordered me to get out of the Ambulance. I got off and gave them space so that they would take my wife down with care. I took a moment to look up to heaven; I knelt down and asked

God for mercy for my wife. While I was praying, I observed some roses, the ones that gave off a very pleasant aroma. I went and cut a rose and handed it to Sue, she took it in her hand and kissed me.

My entire being was exhausted, I walked to the side of the stretcher, but the paramedics told me that I would use the main entrance. I ran to the door as fast as I could and I registered. The receptionist told me; that I had to wait for my wife to be admitted, that it would take approximately 40 minutes. She took me to a waiting room and offered me a cup of coffee. I sat in a chair and turned on the television, to distract my mind. There I waited until they told me that I could go in to see my wife. While I waited, I saw a person dressed in white walking down one of the corridors. I went out to see the person who crossed the door, but the person followed straight ahead and was lost at the end of the corridor. I went back into the room and sat down. I took my backpack and took out my Bible to read it.

I couldn't focus on what I was doing, no matter how hard I tried to control myself, I did not get it. Minutes passed and they did not inform me of my wife's condition, I thought they forgot about me. I went to the Lobby again and asked because they still had not called me, and the receptionist answered because "it's only been five minutes since you arrived here." She saw me so nervous and trembling that she accompanied me back to the waiting room, and helped me to sit in the chair. "Calm down, sir, everything will be fine, go to the garden to breathe fresh air."

She took me to a garden outside the facility, and told me to breathe deeply. I walked through the little garden and took deep breaths to relax. I found a window, and from that window, I could see my wife. When I saw her I felt better. I wanted to be by her side and tell her I loved her. I turned my gaze to another window and saw that the paramedics were covering a woman with a white sheet. The woman looked like the person I had seen walking through the corridors a few minutes ago.

I sat on a stone bench and reflected on what I was living. My mind was lost for a moment, and my gaze was fixed seeing a tree in the center of the garden. I saw an angel that came out from between the plants and walked towards me. I watched him closely, and his face shone like a glow of light. The Angel came and sat next to me, and said; "I will be here by your side until the last breath of your wife. But let me tell you one thing if you do not control your emotions; this process of life will be harrowing for you and your wife." I listened to the Angel, and I reassured myself, although it is not easy to be strong in those moments like that. But at the bottom of my being, I understood that what was happening was inevitable and that only in that way did I see life differently, and this event would be part of my spiritual growth.

I made a promise to the Angel. "And how do you know, if my wife will go to heaven?" He answered saying, "Because I will be the one who will prepare her way before entering the kingdom of God, and you will see it with your own eyes. When she dies and when she is facing God, she will be judged like every human being, but apparently, your wife has been a holy woman for the last seven years." After listening to the Angel's response, I felt better, and the pain I felt in my heart disappeared. The Angel told me; "Let's go see your wife, she is ready to receive us. Do not worry so much, because the spirit of God will be upon us tonight. And he will take the Spirit of your wife, and lead her to heaven."

Thanks to the words of the Angel, I lost my fear and I could also control my emotions. In the company of the Angel, I headed back to the Lobby, and asked for my wife's room number. The Nurse leaned out of her chair and very kindly directed me to my wife's room. At the time of entering the room my wife was happy and said; "I'm waiting for you, my love! Why are you late to arrive?" And before I answered, she noticed the Angel's presence and asked me: "Who comes with you?" I said, "He is an Angel sent by God." She asked me to get close to her, then she whispered in my ear "You

141

are with EDDE right." Then she added to the conversation; he is the Angel that took me to the first surgery at Sunrise Hospital, and He is the same Angel at (St Rose De Lima Hospital) in the second hospital. You know he has revealed to me because he has been with us. But that I will not tell you, you will have to decipher it and understand it with the passage of time. And when you say it, you will be the highest man spiritually on earth, and that will bring you happiness in your life.

What I can tell you; is that he has been taking care of me, since that day I had the embolism. And he has told me so many beautiful things about the kingdom of God that I want to be there. He gave me details of the great city of God. I already want to be there, serving God and being part of his celestial choir. Remember, which is my last wish, the Angel that is here present will be your guide; He will accompany you to the mountain to scatter my ashes. I want to continue being part of nature. Because I am dust and I am converted into dust." After a while, my stepdaughter entered, and ran to hug her mother. I left the room and gave them a moment so that they could say goodbye without interruptions.

When I returned to the room the doctors were already there, they explained to us; what was the procedure to follow, and we agreed as it was the will of my wife. And the doctors gave her the first dosage of Morphine. And they left, they told us that my wife only had one or two hours of life. At that moment my instinct made me take my wife and my stepdaughter by the hand, and we prayed together. I took my Bible in my hands and began to read the book of Psalms; my wife listened very attentively to the reading and closed her eyes.

The injection of morphine was already taking effect. I asked her, do you want me to sing some songs? She asked if I would I sing "Amapola," I would sing the song and my voice would wake her up, and saw me with her eyes full of tears. There was no going back, she had made that decision, and the morphine was already inside her Blood System. I kept singing, I sang more than ten songs that she liked. But her look was the same as it was on our wedding day. Her eyes bright and bright, and her lips a little dry.

After two hours she fell asleep, and we called the doctors to examine her vital organs. After they observed her, they told us that she only slept, her heart was still beating. So the hours passed, and again they injected her with more morphine; now the dose was double. She woke up and asked for a strawberry ice cream and a chocolate cake. She said that was the last thing he wanted to eat before she died. One of the nurses went for the cake and the ice cream, while the rest of the medical group monitored my wife. When they finished applying the second dose, they told us that the dose was already stronger and that now she was not going to wake up. We continue to pray and prepare to give her the cake and ice cream in her mouth. I took a spoon and told my wife to open her mouth to give her some cake.

With a sad look she looked into my eyes, and at the same time, she opened her mouth. I gave her two or three tablespoons of chocolate cake, and I passed them very slowly. She enjoyed her cake so much and then she asked for strawberry ice cream, and I also gave her one spoonful in her mouth. She looked like a baby, and it made me remember that day when my little Brandy passed away to a better life. I could not control my thoughts; I do not know why I found a significant similarity between the two events. Only God knows because he gave me this difficult task, to live these bitter experiences. With all this I have lived, I no longer know how much pain I can tolerate in life. I heard the voice of the Angel in my ear saying; "God will make it up to you in a great way, and your name will never be forgotten in this world. For now, prepare to assist your wife, take your Bible and pray for her; because time approaches the dawn, Sue will be united with God forever."

I tried to enjoy the last moments of my wife's life, every minute for me counted as one day. But the clock did not stop swinging, I continued with my prayers. Within my prayers that I made to God, I asked him to forgive all my wife's sins. That he should receive her in his arms, and let her be part of his heavenly choir. As a good minister and servant of God, I used my talents to comfort, the suffering of my wife.

As expected, my brother-in-law did not show up, he preferred to work than see his sister leave. I can imagine how painful it would have been for him, and for her. I hope he always remembers her as what she was, a Lady in every sense of the word and a good wife. I learned many good things about her, I learned to value the family. She had a phrase that I liked "Charity begins at home," and she was right in what was said. The time continued running, and the hours passed faster and faster. Without feeling the hours go by, it was nine o'clock in the morning. And the doctors again evaluated my wife. The doctors were surprised that my wife was still alive and finally decided to up the dose of morphine to the maximum.

And with that new dosage, she closed her eyes and did not wake up; I took her in my arms, and I hugged her as hard as I could. I did not want to let her go. I wanted time to stop forever. But that was impossible. A few minutes after they injected her, she made a long sigh. This was the most difficult moment of my life, for a moment I felt that I was fainting. The Angel was still present, there he stood beside me and told me. Look at the spirit of your wife going towards the sky and my father God extending his hands to receive her. And I set my gaze, on the body of my wife, and I saw as an aura of white smoke shining as it left my wife's corpse. And I saw it as it slowly ascended into the sky. The Angel went to the side of my wife's spirit. The Angel stopped for a few seconds and told me that God wanted to see me again; on the mountain. And when you go up there on the mountain, God will reveal to you what is your purpose in life.

I saw how the Angel got to heaven, and he reached the spirit of my wife. And the two of them got lost in the sky. I closed my eyes

144

and shouted to the four winds, God has my wife in His holy Glory, Amen.

I turned my gaze, again to the corpse of my wife. And I saw her immobile without life. Her body did not respond to my words anymore, and I asked God for strength so as not to lose heart. I felt the right hand of God on my shoulders and his hand comforted and calmed me down. I heard the voice of God as a whisper in my ear; it was a soft voice telling me, "Your wife Sue is already in my kingdom, dismiss her body and you will fulfill her last wish. My Angels will set you up to make your pain lighter. And I, who am your God, will wait for you on that mountain. Remember that this will be your last meeting with me. Prepare yourself as best you can, so that you climb that mountain. With which you will comply with the last wish of your wife. You will spread her ashes as she asked you in life. And after that, you'll climb to the top of the mountain; where I will be waiting for you in the company of my Angels and Cherubim. For now, resign yourself to go home and rest."

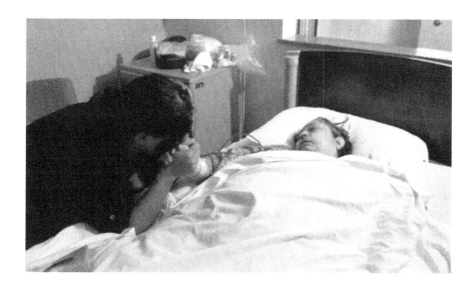

At Las Vegas Nevada, My Wife Sue, EDDE and I

I said goodbye to my wife's body, kissing her, on her forehead and I saw a smile on her face. I left that place and went to my house, driving as carefully as I could, respecting traffic and speed signs. I looked around, felt a big gap in my heart like something was missing. I came home and tried to rest but I could not, in my mind I was following that moment in which my wife passed away. I had no intention to eat, the first night at home, I could not sleep. My thoughts overwhelmed me. I needed comforting. I needed my wife, I needed a hug from someone, and I turned around and did not see anyone, and I asked God for a hug. Because God was the only one accompanying me, during the years of my wife's illness.

I could not sleep so I got out of bed, I could not find tranquility, and I directed myself outside the house to contemplate the stars. But even observing the brightness of the moon and the stars - I had no tranquility. I felt despair that neither my mind nor my body could control. So I spent the night awake, thinking and reliving all those special moments, living with my wife, so many memories and so many joys. Without feeling the hours pass, I saw the first rays of the sun to cross the horizon. In my apartment, I reclined in the chair and fell asleep. While I was sleeping all my dreams were related to Sue. She told me she was not dead. That she only slept and that she was very happy in that eternal dream. When I woke up, I received a call from the funeral home, they told me that they already had my wife's body, and they summoned me to sign the proper documentation for the cremation process.

I went to that appointment and signed all the necessary documents, and the days went by, waiting for my wife's remains. Three days passed until they called me again. Now I was ready, to fulfill my wife's last request. Climb the mountain to honor her memory, and spread her ashes.

Chapter Seven

My Third encounter with God in Las Vegas Nevada.

As a good husband and a man of my word, I could not miss the promise I made to my wife. And the day came to fulfill the last wishes of my wife. Which was to "Spread my ashes on the mountain," and in that place I would have my last encounter with God; thus it was revealed by the Angel Ra-suti-el. And took the portion of my wife's ashes, placed them inside four urns made of clay; each of the Urns had the shape of a heart. And I asked God to be my guide all the way up to that mountain.

Getting Ready to climb up Mountain Charleston with my wife's ashes; my last encounter with God

As I reached that great mountain and climbed with my wife's ashes to the top, I closed my eyes and placed the remains of my wife on the blanket on which there was the image of Jesus Christ. I prepared to pray and ask God for my wife's eternal rest. I fell into a vision with God, and he took me in a dream to a holy place, which was to the east side of a big city with three mountains, and I saw an image of a lion in front of a great mountain, and I saw the name of that beast. And that symbol of the lion with great wings of an eagle would bring like a dream the spirit of my wife before God. And the Angels of God ordered me to make a cave under the figure of the Lion.

I asked the Angels, "Why do you want to do it here and not on fertile land?" And they responded with a voice of authority; "Because here is the main door to eternity, and also because in this place your wife will be baptized, purified, and re-dressed in her new white robe. And after being purified, you will place on her head a golden crown, with seven symbols, which represent the seven Spirits that are in front of the throne of God. And finally we will put on her body, a mantle of purple color with stars and sun shades, and the moon under her feet, and after that, she stands on the moon, and she will be ready to live and reign in the gardens of God.

The Angeles took the urns from my hands, opened them very carefully and threw them into the air, and from the dust, my wife's body was reformed to perfection. And then the Angels of God, placed the body of my wife on a table, and on each corner of the table there was a flame of fire, and in front of the table, there was an offering of bread, water, myrrh and flowers. With much amazement, they proceeded with the preparation of the body and the spirit of my wife, and I rejoiced to see my wife dressed as a virgin!" When the Angels finished preparing my wife, the figure of Lion came to life and my wife was made alive, my wife got up from the table and climbed on the beast and said goodbye to me. But

148

before leaving, she told me; I have a secret to share with you. Listen carefully, "My departure is temporary, but I will return in the last days, and I will give you one last sign in heaven; which is for all of humanity and you will tell them that a new era is already here. But they will refuse to understand, that the era of the Lamb of God is over, and when they hear this message, they will make War, nation against nation, people against people, the slave against the Master, and all will try to exterminate the one against the other; and the rich will want to maintain power over the poor, and the False Prophets along with the False Apostles, will want to keep humanity under false doctrines, created by their primitive minds. But listen carefully to my message; The God of eternity will send you with a jar in your hands, pouring holy water over their bodies and their spirits; to cleanse their sins. And if they do not understand that sign, then there will be fire from the pitcher, and they will burn them all alive or dead, and only then will they know that this is a sign from God. And I tell you; that thus the entrance of the new era will be announced, which belongs to the real Emmanuel (M-anue-L), accompanied by Angel Ra-suti-el.

And that was God's message to you, now I can leave." I promised my wife that every night I would look to the heavens, waiting for that great signal. And I also promised that I would worship Her and God in this Holy place. And I saw how the Lion with great wings took flight through the heavens, and on his back, he took my wife dressed as a Virgin, to the presence of God. Amen.

By living in the flesh the Miracles and the Mysteries of God, I shed a few tears of happiness. And the angels, seeing me cry, came to me to give me words of consolation. And they confirmed what my wife said, saying; "Your wife was not the one who spoke, but the Spirit of God." I just said, "God can use any pure and Holy person filled with the Holy Spirit, to announce a message of salvation to humanity."

After my promises to my wife, I tried to understand why God chose that specific place. Then, the Angel of revelation spoke; "This land belongs to Het-Asar. He is king of the Hittites. And his God of Het-Asar is the same God of Adam, Abraham, Isaac, Jacob, and Moses." I thanked Angel Rasutiel for his explanation, and also thanked him for having abrogated my wife's ashes. And thanks to the message given to me by God through my wife, I understood that the Heteos will be the masters and lords of the new people of God. The seventh hour arrived in the afternoon, and I walked out of the cave, under the figure of Lion. And I fell into a deep sleep for a couple of hours. And in the ninth hour the Angel of revelation woke me up, and he ordered me to sit on a square stone in the shape of a house, and I sat on the stone that he pointed out to me, and the Angel called two women, from the land of the Hittites, to anoint my body. They had alabaster bottles in their hands, one contained myrrh balm and the other perfume, and the two women anointed my feet with myrrh and then perfumed my body. And when they finished, the women raised their hands to worship God and ask Him to be just when judging my heart.

In this way, the Angel Rasutiel prepared me, to enter a tunnel of light which ends in front of the Throne of God. And the Angel told me; when you stand before God, He will reveal to you the mysteries of his kingdom and He will share with you the secrets of the creation of man and the universe. And after all that God shows you, your spirit will be free and you will become a Star of light, as is the Shining Star of the morning, and your name will be written in the book of eternity, and your new name will be equal to that of Angel "Ra-suti-el." And he will take you to the land of Israel and pass through Memphis Egypt and stop at Jerusalem. And when you enter Jerusalem you will bear witness to the Kingdom of God, and all the religious leaders of those lands will be surprised by your testimony and will be the times like the times of Caesar. And the Caesar governor of those lands will be your Judge, and will command you to arrest. For he knows that you are of the lineage of Adam, and that your father is Set-Asar the father of Seth, and also father of the deliverer of the people of Israel, the one who was called King of the Jews. But before you are arrested, an army of Angels will descend from heaven, and they will take you in a sphere-shaped ship, to a sacred place named HEDDEH. And that place is similar to the garden of the EDDEN and there the new city will be established. Which in name will be compared with the city of Jerusalem, and the settlers will say, that it is the New Jerusalem; but the governors of that land, will not understand the message that you bring them, because it is not yet the time for them, to know the truth and reality of their existence.

Although God already commanded you, as a sign to a woman in heaven, upon a beast with the Sun on her head and the Moon under her feet, being persecuted by a great dragon. I know the false Prophets and the false Apostles, and the religious organizations will not understand these signs, because they are distracted by their sins. But God will send you a new sign in heaven, and they will finally understand that we are already in a new era, which will last for 26,000 years. And all this that I say in this book is true, and that truth was revealed by God and his Angels.

After these things happen, come the end of the world and 99% of mankind will perish, and then with the power of God, a new human race with more intelligence and wisdom will resurface out of nothing, and they will be like the Ancient Gods, which inhabited the earth in the days of Cain and Abel. Because God is Love and He will give humanity a second chance, and He will take his new creation back to the Garden of Eden, and he will give them the fruit of the Tree of Wisdom and Eternal Life.

Suddenly, the Angel uttered a few words, in tongues and the sky became cloudy, everything became obscured and there were gusts of wind. Between the gusts of wind, a loud sound was heard. And the power of that sound will be the heavens, and a great white cloud will appear throwing flashes of light. Seven Angels will come down and join in prayer to the Angel Rasutiel. Each of the Angels represents the seven Spirits, who are facing the throne of God, and each of the Angels has a Star in their hands. And those Stars that the Angels possess in their hands are to form the image of him, who resurrected the third day from among the dead, and He is the same who holds the keys of Hades and of eternity.

The Angeles and I continued walking forward on that mountain, and little by little we approach the top. Before arriving at the presence of God, the angel of knowledge ordered me the following: When you enter the Kingdom of God, you will write everything you hear and see in front of God's presence. And I will give you the Title of the last Chapter.

And the Angel named the following chapter. "The sacred book of HEDDEH" And this will be your last chapter in this physical life. After this process, your body and spirit will become a Star, and you will be like the shining MorningStar. And your brightness and radiance will be eternal like God Himself.

Chapter Eight

"The Sacred Book of HEDDEH"

This is the only sacred book, in the world inspired and revealed by the Angel of Wisdom, Truth, and Knowledge. And the Angel came to me with Divine Revelation, by order of the God of Eternity, and in the name of Jesus Christ, His son. The firstborn of the dead. Who on his first day of death, he descended into the darkness and preached to the captives. This message is addressed to all mankind, especially to all those who doubt the existence of God. And also for religious leaders, who are waiting for the second coming of Jesus Christ. Initiating thus the prophecy of the foundation of the new Jerusalem, which is in the land of the Hittites, in the new continent and is in the waiting for its founder, who comes with a pitcher of water in his hands pouring heavenly waters on humanity. He is the absolute owner of the New Era. He is the true M-anue-L sent by God "HEDDEH".

And I asked the Angel, "How do you know, that the new city will be founded in the land of the New Hittites?" And he answered; "Because God likewise has revealed it, and because that is where eternity begins and its door descends from heaven and finally, because in that place there will be no need for the light of the sun or the light of the moon, that's where the celestial and terrestrial waters, are reflected as mirrors and join the two to form the eternal river. And also, that God has already started the foundation of his new people because it was announced by his Prophets. And just as it happened two thousand years ago, when the Jewish people did not recognize Jesus Christ, so it happened with the two witnesses sent by God, M-anue-L and Ra-sutiel; who will be one only in the

153

spirit of God. Those who will be chastised, imprisoned, and massacred by the Religious people. But they will endure all torture of man, because they are full of the Holy Spirit. Unfortunately for any man who will massacre my two Witnesses, because my anger will be spent on all his family and relatives, and as a punishment, I will erase his names from the Book of Life for Eternity. And when my anger pours out on humanity, every sinful man will cry out to the four winds for salvation and justice. They will scream! "God save us! Save all humanity, but they will not die, because God will take them to a place of torment, and their bodies will be submerged in the lake of fire for all Eternity." And after hearing the voice of God, the Angel mentioned the name of the one who comes to found the new Church of God, and the one who brings in his right hand a measuring cane, and in his left hand a pitcher of Water.

I asked the Angel, "What or who is the true Church of God?" And he responded, "Listen carefully son of man, it is very easy to recognize, which is the Church that preaches the truth about all things pertaining to God. To identify the Church, the first thing you have to understand is the following; The kingdom of God is for all those who have consecrated themselves to Him and have taken the name of the Father, the Son, and the Holy Spirit. And concerning who knows the truth about the Kingdom of God; I tell you Son of Man, only a few people know the truth of the kingdom of God. And it is only those who have managed to decipher, the great mysteries of the birth and death of the Lamb of God, which is symbolically repeated, year after year in the heavens in front of the throne of God."

I asked the Angel to give me an example, and he said, "When you enter a church or a temple and ask the Pastors, the Priests, or the Religious Leaders if they know where the throne of God is? And if they know where the throne is, and they show it to you. So it means that they have the truth of things. And if perhaps they know it and they do not teach you the way that means they are false

154

Prophets. But if they do not know where the throne of God is, stay away from them because possibly they worship Satan. And when they worship Satan, they become lovers of material things and money. And as a punishment to their abominations, rain of fire from the heavens will fall on the earth. And the third part of humankind will burn, and a third of its seas and rivers will dry up. And people will run to the mountains to take refuge from the wrath of God. But even hiding in caves will not save them, because they did not repent in time of their sins and their abominations."

This is part of the pure and true prophecy, which God revealed to me in the presence of the Angel Ra-sutiel. And all this that I saw will be fulfilled when I die, at the moment that my Soul separates from my body. And my Spirit will go to the darkness, and there I will feed the dead, and I will also baptize them in the fire. And that will be on the first day of my death, and there I will be waiting for my resurrection, which will arrive on the third day of my departure and will be the date 02-01-2060 of this era. And at the time of my resurrection, the heavens will be opened, and a rain of fire will fall on the earth, and all the prophets will be united, with chants of joy. And all will speak in tongues, like that day of Pentecost.

Until then, I will enter the kingdom of God. And after the new people of God see my resurrection, faith will be restored among the people of God. And the Jew will want to be like Christian and Christian like the Jew and all will be confused and will see the new people of God emerge from nothing. This is how God will reestablish a new order here on earth, and that new people will be of the descendants of the Hittites, and after all these things happen, God, himself will transform me into a Star. And I will be brighter than the shining Morning Star.

All this will take place in the seventh year of the New Era depicted by the great constellation on December 21, 2012. When I was in the city of God, called "Path to God" and looking towards the North of the great city, I saw how a white cloud of heaven descended. And that cloud threw rays of light, and a powerful voice was heard; which mentioned my name. I looked upwards, and I saw the face of an Angel, who leaned out of the cloud, he revealed his name to me (Esq.1: 4), and his name is Ra-suti-el; He told me; "I will be with you for seventy days, and in those seventy days I will prepare your body, your spirit and your soul for death and resurrection. And when I finish with your purification, I will take you in front of the Seven Spirits that guard the throne of God. They will show you how the universe was before the creation of man. And they will also show you the ancient symbols of those events, and those symbols are engraved on the "The Sacred Book of HEDDEH" which God showed you that day in the desert, where you had the first encounter with Him."

These symbols show the right hand of God, ordering all things in the universe and on earth, separating the pure and the impure. Gently forming geometric figures and those geometric figures are the basis and essence, rationalizing the knowledge of man. God created on the earth the figure of a Man, the figure of a circle, a square, and a triangle, followed by a straight line, which extends to infinity, thus indicating time and space. And the hands and the Spirit of God spread over the terrestrial and celestial waters in the direction of eternity. The thoughts of God created everything in the universe; the vibration of his word created the movement in the universe, as a way of accelerating time and space, and the Word was with God.

After this took place and I understood these things, the Angel and I started our journey, and he took my hand and took me up in a cloud to the height of heaven (Ezekiel 8:3). And from above I could see every corner of the square city of God, with its twelve celestial doors.

I also saw three high mountains; it seemed a reflection of what exists up here in the heavens. The Angel confessed to me, that the mountain that is in the middle of the three; is the mountain that

God chose to build his temple, and in front of the mountain is the Lion of the tribe of Judah. And next to that Lion I will be guarding "The Holy Book of HEDDEH" for all eternity.

Next, the Angel and I flew over the city of God, where I walked through the golden streets of that great city and entered its sacred temple and touch with my hands, the throne where the owner of Eternity is sitting. I will walk on the waters of the river, which divides the great city of God. And I will look closely at the brightness of the face of God, which illuminates all the hearts of the afflicted. And we descended for a moment in the center of the big city, and the angel took me in front of two trees, one was the tree of life, and the other was the tree of the wisdom of good and evil. And the Angel gave me to choose which tree I wanted to eat its fruits. I told him that I did not know which was the best of the two, and he gave me the properties of each of the trees; after listening to the Angel, I decided to eat the fruit of the tree of eternal life.

After I ate the fruit of the tree of Eternity, I heard the voice of the Almighty Creator commanded the Angel to "Take me to the desert for seventy days, and to leave me in the company of the Seven Spirits for purification before I can enter His Temple." The Angel obeyed God and took me to the desert in search of the Spiritual site.

And the trip with the Angel Ra-suti-el began. We left the city of God, he took me to the desert of Egypt where Vegetation is scarce, our food was palm dates, and dried meats that the same Angel prepared. And we also drank water from springs that God gave birth to at the foot of the mountains. And he dressed me in white linen gowns that reached to the ground and were brightly illuminated. The Angel gave me a golden staff that looked like bronze. He also gave me a bar to measure, and a linen string with colored stones; blue and white (Ez 40: 3); He put on my chest a gold sash which illuminated colors like the rainbow. He also covered me, with a leopard skin coat to withstand the cold; and finally, He gave me golden sandals to walk on the desert sand.

Afterward, the Angel dressed me up, he ordered me to raise my hands as a sign of prayer, to worship God in front of an altar full of offerings. And the offerings were; bread, wine, oil, fruit, flowers, and incense. I raised my hands, and suddenly I saw the sun rising in my arms. The Angel kept walking beside me and spoke in my ear to tell me to continue forward. And as I walked a little more, I saw two women; each of them had a symbol on their head. The first symbol looked like a figure on a throne, and the second symbol looked like a cup. And the two women were kneeling on cushions made of gold, and they looked at each other in the eyes as the sun rose towards the sky. And its rays of the Sun illuminated their faces. And on one side of the two women, there were six Spirits of God; singing like a choir of Angels in harmony with the two women. They sang "Holy, Holy is the Lord, who lives and reigns forever and ever, Amen."

I continued on my journey with the Angel. I came to a place where twelve Elders were sitting on twelve thrones. And each one of them had in his hands a golden staff, and two of them had in their hands the Divine light of God. It looked as if the rays of the Sun dressed them. And in front of the twelve elders, opened a table which had an offering of bread, wine, oil, and incense. And when we passed in front of the twelve elders, one of them got up from his throne, and I heard him say; "I am the Re-ey of the New Hittites the first of the house of HEDDEH, and I am the guard of the first heavenly gate."

Standing in front of this elder man there was a figure of a scorpion, and the elder told me; quietly; "Today you will be judged by God, and your verdict depends on the works of your heart. I continued walking, I entered a corridor, and I stopped in a room that was full of light. And I arrived in front of two beings, those whose faces were covered. One of them had the aspect of a lion and the second had the appearance of a bird. And I saw in the hands of the one who looked like a bird, a list of all my works. And being with the appearance of a lion, holding a scale with both hands. And being with the appearance of a lion, holding a scale with both hands. Behind the scales, I did reach to see a Dragon devourer of a death. The dragon had seven horns and teeth similar to the teeth of a crocodile.

When it was the time of my judgment, an Angel dressed in green put the list with all my works, inside a clay vessel in the shape of a heart. And the vessel was placed on one side of the scale, and on the opposite side of the scale was a dove. That dove represents the Holy Spirit of God. The elders called me again, and I approached them, and one of the elders said, "All of us were, we are, and will be Kings upon the land of God." And this elder was occupying the second throne in front of the balance. And that same elder asked me another question, "Who are you?" And I answered with a voice of command;

"I am the yesterday, the today and the tomorrow, I am the one who is born and I am the one who dies, again and again, every day, and my spirit is like that invisible force, the one that created God and God gave me power, to feed those that rest in the beyond. And I am that master of the resurrection because my body will be reborn and resurrected on the third day of my death. I am the one who drives the heavenly boat of the all-powerful, I am full of Divine Light because I am with God and God is with me, because I am that 'Path to God' and I am the one who guides and helps souls, to ascend in the celestial firmament. I am the radiation of the Glory of God, and the invincible force that is within my spirit; it is the same force united to God's. I am the one with the double Spirit, God's and mine; I am the essence of the celestial water coming from of God, which is poured out by the owner of the new age, and that water comes from my ancestors of the city Ra-Ka-Mu.

I am that shining Morning Star. I am a light of energy, which illuminates the world. And I am that same light that dwells within all beings, and I am the son of the eternal God."

After saying all these words inspired by God, the twelve elders were removed from their thrones, and came before me and prostrated themselves before the throne of God. And I remained immobile until I heard my final verdict. Without knowing why, my eyes filled with tears, and memories of my life were flashing through my mind. For a moment there was total silence and I felt that my life was extinguished. But at the end of my judgment, they determined that my works were equally balanced with the spirit of God, and the dragon of death cannot devour me.

When the twelve elders heard my verdict, they got up from the floor and embraced me. They cried with joy and told me; you are a righteous person with a good heart, that's why your works are pure, and that has saved you, and finally, they said; "That Angel who always accompanies you, today he will take you in front of the throne of God." After listening to the twelve elders speak, the Angel and I continued on our way, and we arrived at another part of the tunnel. We came to another room full of light, where there were four beings in front of a throne. And those living beings are the children; of him who sits on the right hand of God. The four beings have wings, and they sit in front of the throne. And they walked straight ahead, guarding the throne where he sits, one with the figure of a man. And in his back to the one who sits on the throne, there are two women there. And one of the women had a child in her arms, and she is dressed with the Sun. And she has the moon under her feet and on her head a crown with twelve stars. (Rev. 12:1).

And the two women have symbols on their heads, these two women are the same as I saw at the entrance of the tunnel, and they are also the same, who anointed me with perfume and myrrh. Under the throne, I saw the ark of the covenant of God, that ark will be consecrated, for the new people of God. And I asked God for wisdom to understand his new covenant. This new covenant between God and his people will be only for those who have consecrated themselves to God. Because the new salvation of humanity depends on their faith, and their obedience to God. I heard a shuddering voice that said; "Son of man look at the ark of the covenant and the symbols that are above it" I looked, and I read the symbols; "THREE THINGS FOR THE NEW COVENANT WITH GOD." and then, "FAITH, LOVE, OBEDIENCE."

I walked toward the Ark of the Covenant. And the same voice commanded me to open the Ark of the new covenant, and when I opened it, flashes of light came out, and there were thunder and lightning. I could see the contents of the ark; something wonderful and glorious. It was Priest's clothing cast with gold and precious stones, and then God ordered me to wait with Angel Ra-sutiel to receive the Ark of the Covenant.

While waiting for God to give me the Ark of the Covenant, I looked up from the throne of God, and in the highest part of the throne, I saw twelve snakes that were next to an Eagle. And the eagle had huge wings, spreading as if getting ready to fly. Each of the serpents represents a heavenly gate, which opens and closes one at a time. And soon I saw how the eagle started its flight and rose so high in the sky it disappeared, the twelve serpents closed their celestial doors so that no one enters or leaves the great city of God.

No one will enter for a period of time until the new covenant is sealed between God, I and his new people. And the new covenant will be closed, before the presence of the children of God. And the son of God will be given him the keys of his kingdom, to his successor, the owner, and Lord of the New Era. He is coming from the sky, with a pitcher of water in his hands. And the priests of these times will not recognize it now, and will not until the144th year of this new Era. And the children of the Lamb of God will rejoice when these things come to pass.

Each of the four Gospels of the Bible is represented by Gods four children who sit in front of the throne. And I saw the four sons of the lamb, they have the form of humans from head to toe, but their heads were like beings from other places. And the first had the face of a man, the second face of a lion, the third face of an ox and the fourth a face of an eagle, and the four beings just walked straight, as if the spirit of God was leading them forward. I knelt before the four beings, to praise the one who was sitting on the throne. And in his hands of the one who was sitting on the throne, I saw a measuring staff. And when he spoke his voice was like a swarm of bees, and his eyes were like flames of fire.

He who was sitting on the throne ordered me to get up so that I could see the crowd that was walking towards the new city. And all the people were carrying their belongings. They were already prepared to live and found that new city. Which was promised to them, by God himself and was written in his sacred writings? And all believers in God came in search of paradise. Similar to the old Jerusalem, with twelve doors that has one of the twelve elders sitting in front of each entry.

And that great crowd is the group of the 144,000 called by God (Rev. 7: 4) and they all carry the seal of God on their foreheads, and when they finish entering the city of God, until then the heavens will be open with rain of fire from heaven, and the four sons of the lamb will speak in tongues, and the ark of the covenant will be in the center of the great city of God. And the people of God will sing praises of joyfulness, and they will carry the Ark of the Covenant on their shoulders, and walk with it to the new city of "HEDDEH."

When the children of God arrive with the Ark of the Covenant to the New Land, after arriving in the city of God; all the nations will start a war on the children of God, and the four beings that stand in front of the throne of God, in the company of the seven angels will protect the 144,000 who are sealed. They will guide them to the New Jerusalem, which is already established in the land of

162

the New Hittites, the new land will be governed by its leader the owner of the new age, the one who holds a water jar in his hands. And he will be seated in a throne inside a white house full of light.

Then the Angel ordered me to open my mouth, and he gave me a piece of rolled paper, on which were written the names of the Seven Spirits, I won't speak and eat it; I closed my eyes and felt a bitter taste in my mouth. At the moment of passing the paper down my throat, a vision of God came to my mind. I saw around me many eyes that watched me while eating the paper; I only saw the eyes embedded in stone columns. They made a strange movement, the eyes flared with fire, and those eyes terrified me and my body trembled and sweated with dread. But to hear the voice of God calm me, and the voice of God was so strong, that the eyes that were embedded in the columns fell away.

Suddenly, the divine light of God illuminated the eyes that were still embedded in the columns, and the eyes followed the light that emanated from the top of the sky. Then I heard a proverbial roar from heaven; it was a voice that said; "Do not fear son of man the alpha and the omega is with you; and nothing and no one can harm you, because you are my faithful servant and you have a mission to fulfill on earth. And when you pass to eternal life, I will transform you into a Star." When I heard this, I fell as like a dead man to the ground, and when the angel spoke again with a loud voice he took me to a dark room with columns of gold and boxes of Jade on stones tables.

In the main entrance of the chamber, I found one of the twelve elders, staying vigilant in the main entrance of the chamber. This would be the third elder, inside the chamber there was a stone table made from crystallite, and the Angel placed me on the stone table; then he called forth the Seven Spirits and had ordered them to pray for me. I close my eyes to pray for the world and the salvation of all the captives.

163

Once I finish praying, I opened my eyes, and I saw seven stars at my feet. I also saw my body above the stars. These are the stars that kept my spirit in motion. The Angel confessed to me, that here in this sacred place, the spirit of God multiplies on its own. In the corner of the chamber, I saw a swan with a woman and two small eggs, and I asked her, "What powers do you possess here?" She answered, "I am the symbol of this holy place."

Afterwards, the woman and the Swan disappeared from my sight. I closed my eyes, and I heard the voice of two women. When the Angel ordered me to open my eyes, I saw a woman in the company of her sister, and both sisters kneeled down beside my body, and one of them put her hand on my head, and exclaimed; "Allow my sister to serve you in what she can, and let her open your mouth to eat the best of your offering to God!"

Once they were done partaking part of the offering, they walked away, and then entered the Spirits and prayed for me. Each and every one of the spirits became a star, and my body was united with theirs to form a single body, and at the same time, we joined the body of God. Afterward, the Angel and the spirits formed a circle around the table. Then I saw an army of Angels descend from the heavens. The Angels had in their hands ribbons of many colors, like a rainbow; then they started to wrap my body with the ribbons. The chants from the Angels and the rhythm from God was one. I felt his vibes and his energy within my being. The Angels were dancing around me, and they put ointment perfume in my body that felt like hot honey.

The Angels continued with the ritual and also they sang praise with one voice. The chant of the Angels exalted my heart, to such an extent that their beats sounded like a small drum. I saw that the Angels had candles in their hands, to illuminate my body and they were dancing around me. The Angels didn't cease to sing, "Holy, Holy are you HEDDEH, Holy is the Son of God." The Angels and the seven Spirits anointed my body with perfume. At the same time, one of the Spirits placed a gold coin on each of my eyes lids, the coins were marked with the name of God. "HEDDEH"

They placed in my hands a pair of the golden key to open the doors of Hades; and Heaven. Then Angel Ra-suti-el ordered me to open my mouth, and he placed one scroll in the inside of it. He said, "What is written on the scroll is a secret, and you won't be able to read it, until after the seventy days of your spiritual purification." Then he ordered me to stick my tongue to my palate and seal my mouth with a gold thread. This way I would remain silent for several days. (Ez 3:26), and he also gave me a small metal in the form of a cross with a circle on it. And lastly, he placed in my hands a golden cane and a string with colored stones. And that's how they prepared my body the second time.

When the Angels finished with my preparation and purification, I heard a loud potent voice. It was the voice of God that sounded like thunder. Suddenly, the door sealed in the room where I was placed. I felt like I was being baptized in fire. It was a fire coming from the throne of God. After my baptism in fire, the Angel prepared me for my final purification, he took me to the desert to meet the seven Spirits. And we arrived at that desert where the seven Spirits were in inhabiting, and the Angel called them by name, and one by one, they appeared out of thin air. And once all the Spirits revealed themselves, they showed us a star with their name written on them.

The Angel recognized them and told them what the plan of God was, at that moment, they understood what their mission would be. I was with each of the seven Spirits for ten days each, and each Spirit revealed to me their divinity in their Church. I asked the seventh Spirit, "What will be the sign that will announce my arrival in this new era?" He responded, "Come, walk by my side, and I'll show you the sign." He took me by way of vision to a place where a woman was lying down by the edge of a river, and around her was a lot of dead fish. Also, there were two jackal dogs killing and eating fish. I could not help the woman because her body was already purified. Then the Spirit said this; "Maybe now you might not understand the mysteries of God, but for now, you don't interrupt the coming of the New Era."

When the Spirit finished with that thought, I saw how in the tenth celestial door descended a woman with a water jar in her hands. And the pitcher spilled springs of celestial waters. And the woman poured the waters over the fish, and over the woman lying down on the edge of the river.

Here lies wisdom, and whosoever has ears simply open them and listen. Those who have eyes, open them and watch the vision of God announcing the new era. It will be something similar to what Jesus Christ said, "And that will be wherever the dead body is, there the waters will gather," (Matthew 24:28)

Lastly, the seventh Spirit said this; "I know the works of your heart, and that's why I showed you the vision of the new era; that revelation, guard for yourself, and you will tell no one these things. Because religious people don't believe in the prophecy of God." And that's how the seventy days with the seven Spirits was complete.

The seventh Spirit took me back to the chamber where I was resting. Before I said goodbye, the Spirit said this; "The twelve elders will be opening their celestial doors, so you can enter their homes and have supper with them." Once I arrived in the chamber where my body lay, the Angel Ra-suti-el told me, "Follow me, it's necessary that we continue our journey toward the throne of God. And so we journey through the gardens where there were two holy water pools. I saw two people washing their hands in, and I also saw two tigers lying next to a door, they were entangled together in a skylight quite like the sun. And close to them, two birds with two symbols, one of them was a throne; and the other was a chalice.

The Angel had commanded me to stand in between the two birds with symbols. I did this very carefully so as not startle the birds; as we continued our journey and arrived on the other side of the garden. And on that side were two crosses made of wood. And I sat on a bench to rest for a while, suddenly the four beings that were in front of God's throne appeared.

The four beings inscribe symbols on the bench, and the Angel got close and demanded the significance of the symbols, but the four beings left without saying a word. So I got up from the bench and proceeded with the journey. We left to a place where we saw a figure of a lion, lying in front of a great mountain. And the lion was in front of a celestial door. The one which belongs to the fourth elder and the elder got up from his throne to sit next to the lion.

Behind the lion, there were some plants and a snake. And from that place, I could see from the distance more celestial doors, eight in total, and within those eight doors I must enter them all, before arriving at the throne of God, and it will be twelve celestial doors total I will visit. The elders of each door will deliver me a message in which will help me to achieve eternity. Because when I arrive before God, he will ask me; "What the messages were about from the elders?"

One of the messages from the fourth elder was as follows; under my celestial door, Israel was founded, known as the tribe of Judah, also the lion represents that tribe. And the elder invited me inside his home, and in his house, I saw many beings unknown to me. They appeared to be mutants, and all of them had feathers on their feet and golden thorns on their heads. And I was a bit traumatized by their appearance but the Angel calmed me down. Suddenly I saw two beings coming out of a door, and they had many eyes, and the eyes dispersed rays of bright light; blinding white light, I closed my eyes for a moment, and when I opened them, the two beings were already right before me.

They attempted to take me by hands and I could not resist it. I let them guide me though a secret chamber, but the Angel commanded I let myself be guided by those beings. Because their mission is to take me to the next stage; in which I will find myself in another world. But one of the beings had his head covered and looked like a jackal. And I allowed myself to be guided by those beings, but just a few steps before entering the chamber, one of the two beings opened my mouth with an instrument made of gold and gave me a piece of bread to eat.

That bread has been the sweetest, and most delicious bread I have eaten. Afterwards I entered the chamber, and inside the chamber there was the being with the form of jackal. I continued waling; and in front of him, I saw a crown made of flowers over an Ark. Then the living being and I boarded the Ark, and he I asked me; "Why do you carry that Urn in the shape of a heart?" I responded, "Because it contains the list of all my works." He reviewed my list, and he himself placed my Urn over the table in the custody of the four Angels.

The Angels were sitting on a boat by the lake. Then the Angels helped me get into the boat, and we crossed the lake. Once arriving in the other side, I recline on a table, and then a dove descended over my body and placed an amulet in the shape of an omega over my abdomen. And this house belongs to the Fifth Elder, and the Elder is seated on his throne, dressed in white linen.

The Spirit of God and his Angel continued guiding me, in between those celestial doors, preparing me for the arrival of the New Era. Later I enter through another celestial door. It's the door of the Sixth Elder, and in that house, I saw The Spirit of God in the form of a dove. I saw how the same dove flew to the highest of heaven. And descended at very fast speed, and then disappeared into the depths abyss.

Then the Angel took me by the hand, and we crossed the abyss using a bridge. And on the other side of the bridge, we found a pair of twins dressed as priests; they had red candles in their hands, which blinded my sight. So I continued walking until I entered another chamber; where I found another Elder sitting on his throne, he got up on his feet and gave me a cane, so I kill the serpent that was hiding inside one of the pots. Then after the serpent was diminished a white dove appeared on a boat. The Angel commanded me to board the boat with the dove, so that we could sail through the heavens and the stars; because that dove will take me to the next house where Seventh Elder sat in his throne.

Once I entered the seventh house, the Angel commanded that I raise my hands to pray, and when raised my hands in praise, a light illuminated the corner of the chamber. In that corner, I saw a throne. Sitting on that throne I saw someone dressed in white linen, his hair was white as snow, and his eyes were of sapphire. And that being was accompanied by a woman, the woman had a crown on her head, and she raised her hands in prayer.

And I saw at the roof of the throne seven serpents, in which they were embedded to the roof of the throne. I asked the Angel for an explanation on the meaning of these serpents, and he said; "Right now is not the time for you to understand these things." I walked a bit more throughout the house, and then I saw a beast lying on the floor with big horns, with a bit of fear I got close to the beast, and I saw that it was a bull, with the sun over his head.

I passed by this beast and left for the next house, the Angel came with me, and we went into the Eighth House together. Then the elder of that house received us and invited us to enter his house. Once inside I observed a bronze floor and walls made of silver, with stairs guarded by golden rams, and at the end of the room a golden throne, where the owner of that house was seated. I saw his name carved on a stone, but the Angel asked me not to pronounce that name. And the old man who was on the throne had a white robe and in his hands a golden staff.

I made myself cautiously to see the elder up close, but a voice disturbed me, and we quickly left the room, in the courtyard of the house there was a crowd of Elders. They were sitting on square stones, and there were twenty-four Elders in all, and in front of the elders I saw two beasts lying on a stone, and the first beast was a ram with wings, and the second beast was an ox with a sun on its head. And the angel spoke in my ear and told me the meaning of the two beasts. These beasts represent the two previous Eras, the Era of the Lamb of God; to whom the Ninth House belongs.

I asked the Angel, "What is the symbol of the ninth House?" And the Angel answered, "A couple of fish or two fishermen with their Master called the Messiah, also known as the Fisherman of men, or the Lamb of God." And after that I understood the meaning of this sign, we continued on the boat and crossed the sky. And the Angel said. "It is time for us to descend from heaven because it is almost time for your last encounter with God. And in the company of the seven spirits I will prepare you for that moment; but first, we will pass over a river, we will go in search of the two fishermen representing the Ninth House."

With the power of God, we descended from the celestial waters, that formed a powerful current, and finally we landed over the terrestrial waters, here we met the two fishermen, and the Angel called the fishermen by name, and they recognized his voice and invited us to board their boat. We boarded their boat and crossed the Great River that divides the city of God, and during the trip on the turbulent waters of the river, the fishermen threw their nets to fish and did not catch anything, because the currents were very strong.

I ordered them to take out the nets and I touched them with my hands, and I asked God to stop the movement of the waters, and the water of the river was calm. And then I ordered the fishermen to throw the nets again into the river. And they left the nets inside the river for eight minutes, and then I gave the signal to the fishermen, to remove the nets of the river; when they took them out, they were full of fish. And the fishermen marveled and knelt in the boat, to thank God; they understood that this was the sign of the new Era.

We reached the other side of the river, and the fishermen were still amazed, and as a thank-you, they invited us to dine at the table of their master the "Messiah." And that miracle was the sign of God for the fishermen. God knew how to announce, the final times of the Age of His son the Messiah. As it happened with Abraham, Moses, and Daniel era; now is time for the age of the Lamb of God to end. But God also knows that when the last days of the Messiah are over, the people of the world will not know what to do. The religious man will enter into confusion and will not accept the will of God, but at the end of time they will understand God's will, and they will accept his new Redeemer. Who by name is Ra-suti-el and is also known as the true M-anu-L, (Emmanuel) as told by the Elders of the city of God.

After meditating a little on what happened, the fishermen asked us to follow them, and they walked by desolate lands, and we arrived at a house on the right of a Synagogue. And when we entered the home of the fishermen, I saw the Son of God dressed in white linen, and his hair was white as snow. And the Son of God dwells with his disciples in the ninth heavenly house, and the entrance to his door is on the side where the sun is hidden.

When the Son of God saw us enter, he sat down at the table and invited us to sit with Him. And in the company of those who directed the boat of God, we sat down to dinner with The Son of God. The Angel spoke with the Lamb of God in tongues, and the inhabitants of that house did not understand what they said, but the Spirit of God gave me the power to understand everything. And the Son of God told the Angel this; "Resignation for the Lamb and a Hallelujah for the one that comes after my Era, He will come with his pitcher in his hands pouring holy water over humanity, and He will bring new teaching, that teaching is Repentance. Because that is how it is written in the book of God."

And the Angel answered, "He who comes with the pitcher in his hands, will dine at your table, and in the presence of your disciples, you will give him your throne and the keys to the doors of his celestial house. The new Son of God represents the Tenth heavenly House, and He will be, The Savior of the New Hittites and will dwell with them in a new continent, the New Jerusalem Hallelujah. The Jew, The Christian, and the Protestant will detest him; for he will be the new redeemer of humanity, and his task is to cleanse the roads to eternity, over which the corrupt, the deceivers, the false prophets and the religious lovers of money and power will not walk. All these groups know beforehand that they are not part of the new covenant with God."

The Lamb of God, I affirm what was said by the Angel, I know that he is the founder of the New Jerusalem. And his grace comes from the celestial waters, which join the earthly waters in the new continent. In this new land is where "HEDDEH," the God of new Hittites dwells. And after hearing all this, the moment came when the Lamb invited us to celebrate the holy supper, and so said the lamb before sitting down at the table: "Son of God, you are like me, a great servant of God, my Father, because I know the good works of your heart, I tell you; Your Era will be better than mine, because for this time humanity has a better understanding of the Divine. And I say unto you that tonight, you won't spend another day without first seeing the face of my Father. I will show you part of my Father's kingdom because that way the prophecy will be fulfilled, written by my servant John on the Island of Patmos."

And the son of God called his successor, and the Angel Ra-suti-el stood up and asked, "My Lord, your Era is over?" And the Lamb answered; "My Era and my time are unknown to the ordinary man, but my successor knows, that my time is over because my father God revealed it to him." The Angel replied; "My Lord, it will be convenient, that among your disciples you said; who is your successor. Just remember that the human heart is evil?"

So answered the Lamb of God; "I can't do anything, except my father's will. Let us close our eyes to pray, and then I will sit down

172

next to my successor so that there is no doubt among my Disciples. And all the guests closed their eyes at the same time to pray, and at the end of the prayer, I opened my eyes and looked at the man sitting next to me, he spoke and said, "Get up son of God, so that my disciples know; who is the one who entered the new Era. My father chose you, and when you enter your Era, you will sit next to that Elder, who watches the door of the new city. And before my time passes, the two Fishermen will be flogged by the unbelievers. And that will be the last sign that I will give to the Jews, the Gentiles and all the Religions of the whole world."

And the Lamb shared his table and his food with the Angel and me, and then he said aloud; "I will be present to see, how the Spirits dress you as a Priest, with a leopard skin over your shoulders, to guide your Spirit in the presence of my Father in the lands of eternity, "HEDDEH" Amen, and the leopard skin will be like Elias's mantle, to protect your path between the earth, the waters and the heavens."

After dinner, the Lamb called the Seven Spirits and ordered them to bring my sacred clothes. And the Lamb of God closed his door and then sealed it with a golden padlock. Then He wrote a name on my body, and named me his successor like Petra was. Thus began my preparation in the presence of the Angel and the Lamb. The Spirits ordered me to lie down on top of a stone table and lit two candlesticks. And since I already had color ribbons attached to my body, it was easier for them to dress me as a Priest.

The garment is the following, the breastplate, the ephod, the tunic embroidered with gold threads, the miter and the belt. (Ex. 28: 4-16), and having the dress ready, the Spirits placed in my body the mantle, my clothes were different red, blue, purple and crimson. And my breastplate was made with gold, blue, green and red precious stones, and the breastplate had a strange shape, it looked like an eagle spreading its wings, and in each wing it had the name of the twelve elders, these are the twelve doors of the new city of

173

God. And the Holy Spirit brought my garment, which was inside the Ark of the Covenant.

The Ark was full of pure gold, and on the outside, it had many symbols, and badges with the names of my ancestors and of the Spirits that accompanied me on my endless journey. As soon as the Angels had the Ark of the Covenant on their hands, there were flashes of light and lightning, and I was frightened and my body shuddered, but the Lamb calmed me down and said, "Fear not Son of God, your clothes are what produce that flash of light" and the Lamb sealed the first door of my house with letters of gold.

He took in his hands a second breastplate of pure gold, with the figure of two fish on the banks. Then he said; "This pectoral belongs to me, and today I place it on your body, so that the power of the Holy Spirit may accompany you in your New Era."

Then the spirits put a bracelet on each of my wrists, the bracelets were made of gold and decorated with precious stones, and symbols similar to eyes, and the eyes seemed to come alive as I saw them blinking and throwing flames of fire. I was terrified to see these things, but the Spirits calmed me, to continue with the preparation of my body. A few minutes later, I listened to the Angel and the Lamb pray over me.

The Angel approached me and he took my right hand, he placed colorful rings on my fingers. And each of the rings represented a Spirit, and their names were engraved on the rings. Also in my left hand, he placed two more rings, and the first had a figure of a scorpion and the second ring had the figure of a beetle. I asked the Angel, "What is the meaning of these rings?" And the Angel answered, "One of those rings represents God's unmistakable self-creating force, the second ring represents the house of the people of the new land; and its main gate on the other side of the celestial river, where the Sun is hidden."

Then, the Angel brought two earrings, and he put them in my ears. And what I saw the next was more astonishing to me, the Angel brought a crown with two pieces, one piece was white and the second was red, and in front of the crown were two figures, the first was a bird and the second looked like a snake, and again I asked the Angel, "What is the meaning of these symbols?" He whispered in my ear the meaning. The hours passed, and my body began to dehydrate, caused by the heat that made from the intense light where I was, and I asked for water to drink, but the Angel told me that I could not eat or drink anything, and continued to pray for my soul and my body. Finally, I was introduced into a vault of pure gold, and inside I saw many badges and symbols. And little by little I felt how the vault embedded itself in my skin.

For a moment everything went silent, I did not hear anything, I saw nothing, and I shouted with great desperation, and my screams were useless because nobody heard me. And suddenly I felt a movement, four beings said my name and said to me, "We will carry you on our shoulders, facing the throne of God. I did not resist and let them carry me, and they brought me before the throne of God. And when we arrived in front of the throne, I saw a throne of pure gold, and one who was sitting there, and his face emanated a shining light that blinded my sight.

And I contemplated his appearance for a moment, and my eyes cried tears of blood to see who is sitting on the throne, and his voice mentioned my name. Afterward, He stood up, and I saw his white garment decorated with blue, green and red stones, and his crown was white with golden bands on the edges. And finally, He ordered me to come near Him, and my body felt heavy, and so my spirit came out of my body, and God said to me; "This time you entered my Kingdom, and here you will dwell for eternity. Your work in physical life is over, and your new spiritual age is just beginning, and by my side, you will be brighter than the Morning Star.

When your Spirit leaves your body, the inhabitants of the earth will see it inert, fainted on a stone. And curse my name on your body, with mocking words. But one year after your death, they will recognize that you are my beloved son and that you lived temporarily on earth, to experience life, death, and resurrection. And the world will shed blood in your name, and wars will be waged, nation against nation, and the false prophets and apostles will cry out for mercy. And they will ask for clemency for humanity, but my anger will be upon them. And a third of the inhabitants will die, because of their wars and their injustice. But I tell you, my son, that the inhabitants of the earth are not worthy of my Kingdom.

Now that you are here at the entrance of my Kingdom; I will reveal to you what will happen to the Elders of the last two celestial doors. They will wait with tranquility, for your Era of dominion over humanity to pass, and they will be filled with joy when it is their turn to govern. But all this will remain secret between you and me, and you will not reveal the identity of the Elders of the last two houses. The work revealing their identity will be of the coming Prophets. They will be guided by my Spirit, and they will wait for their time until this new agreement has completed, that I have just spoken of, and with the new city that is found in the new continent. And now the time has come for you to enter your abode, and take the place of the Lamb. And I, your God, "HEDDEH" will witness your triumphant entrance to your Era, which will reign over the living and the dead."

The Spirit of God took me to my final resting place, which is on the celestial river and it divides the gardens of the city of God. And then I felt how God touched my head with a measuring rod, and he told me, "This is the sign of my new covenant, all those who surrender to my name must be baptized by my servants, my priests or my leaders. And you will also tell them, that repentance is my new mandate. And finally celebrate the holy supper, with bread

176

and wine. And during the dinner, their heads will be touched with a rod of gold.

This ritual is the representation of my Dominion over their Souls. Amen. And I will give you the measures of the rods, which are made of pure gold, so that they may be sacred. And they will also carry a badge with my new name; which is "HEDDEH" that comes from the ancient Hittites. It's already late for you to enter your abode, which will be sealed with my name. And outside the door of your house, I will place four Cherubim, so that they can observe the four corners of Heaven.

The Cherubim will be accompanied, by four virgins, dressed in purple and with gold crowns. And each Virgin will have a symbol upon their forehead; the first Virgin will have a Serpent on her head, the second Virgin will have a Scorpion, the Third Virgin will have a Throne and the fourth Virgin will have a Chalice. And all these symbols will be cast in pure Gold because gold represents the purity of the Spirit, and its brightness will illuminate your dwelling day and night. And also all the walls of your house will be covered with golden paper sheets and the door will be made of granite stone and will have a cello with your name written in Gold.

The Virgins will be guarding the four corners of the earth, the North, the South, East, and West. And they will extend their arms to protect your home, and they will also cover your face with a sacred mask, carved and polished in gold which will protect your identity. Only God, my Angels, my Cherubim, my Seven Spirits, my Four Beings, and my Four Virgins, know who you are. I put you in this house because you are my beloved son. And if anyone desecrates your house, he will be punished with all my wrath, and all his descendants will die suddenly. Now the time has come to seal your house, which is within my Kingdom and is part of the new city that is one side of the EDDEN. This is your last meeting with your God "HEDDEH" The God of eternity, and my Cherubim and my seven Spirits will guard every word in this book."

At last the final words came to me, and He said, "I tell you; nobody can add or take things from this book, only you will do it when the time is right. And if it were necessary to add something, I will come to your house and reveal my commands. Until then, my revelation remains for you and your new people speak good things about my kingdom and protect this book with your life."

And after God said goodbye to me, the Angel entered the room of intense light where I was and told me; "Look around you, here you have everything you had in life, and also everything necessary for your resurrection, which will be this dawn." And when the Angel finished speaking, the sky was open, and I saw a great explosion among the stars, and its light illuminated my entire being. And fireballs were shot into the river that divides the city of God, and its inhabitants were filled with joy, seeing that I ascended to the heavens in a ship and I sat on the right side of the King of the New

Hittites. And so it was my last encounter with God. "HEDDEH"...

Amen, Amen and Amen. I saw all of God's Kingdom in the vision given to me by God alone. Amen.

Made in the USA
Middletown, DE
02 March 2022

62017319R00109